REDEFINING LOVE

CHANGE THE WAY YOU LOVE.
CHANGE YOUR LIFE. CHANGE THE WORLD.

SARA BETH WALD

Content
EMPOWERED

ISBN: 979-8-9877930-0-8 (Paperback)
ISBN: 979-8-9877930-1-5 (Ebook)

The Mission of Redefining Love:
To heal our culture by healing our trauma,
one individual at a time

For my teachers:
Gram, Brenna, Jan, and Sid

And to Isaac and the boys,
with love

CONTENTS

Foreword by Karen Grosz ix

Prologue: How I got here xi

I. AN INTRODUCTION TO REDEFINING LOVE
    1. A New Definition of Love   3

    2. How Do I Redefine Love?   12

II. THE THREE PILLARS
    3. The Three Pillars   25

    4. Boundaries   29

    5. Accountability   39

    6. Grace   57

III. APPLYING THE PRINCIPLES
    7. Forgiveness   63

    8. Speak the Language   69

    9. Dealing with Anger   74

    10. The Shame Cycle   84

    11. Toxic Relationships   90

IV. MAKING CONNECTIONS
    12. The Health Connection   101

13. The Family Connection   117
14. The Friend Connection   123
15. The Romance Connection   131

Epilogue.................................135

Acknowledgements 141

Notes.......................................143

About the Author 147

FOREWORD

IT IS A DISTINCT HONOR FOR ME TO BE ASKED TO write the foreword for *Redefining Love* on many levels. First, because I am an ardent fan of the author and her skill at the keyboard. Sara could write an essay about the dust on my windowsill, and I would be enthralled.

Singer and actor Tim McGraw once said, "I'm not a great singer, but I am an *honest* singer." I hear that honesty in every song he sings, and that is how I think of Sara—*honest*. Not just in her words but because her words sound exactly like her.

She is not putting on airs or inserting stories that are more dramatic than the actual events. She simply and honestly tells her story. There is a warm catalyst for self-acceptance and dramatic change hidden in her beautiful sentences.

Second, I love that I am writing a foreword. My life's mission is to use my creativity and positivity to help teams and individuals move forward. If I were to be honest, as Sara exemplifies, that is probably because I do not want to look back. I do not want to wallow in or even admit to the pain.

I am not as adept as Sara at dealing with snot bubbles. (That's an inside joke that references what Sara calls an "ugly cry.") I have spent my entire adult life living and writing about one *next* and then another, pushing myself and others forward, onward, and upward, without the grace to look in the rearview mirror.

I know this is not always healthy. I know that if I used, as Sara suggests, boundaries, accountability, and grace with myself, I could grow bigger, faster, and further forward.

I teach and accept boundaries, accountability, and grace with the teams and leaders I work with. I even suggest I use them with myself. However, as a flawed human trying to love myself at all costs, I can admit here that until I read this book, I did not pay enough attention to the possibility of truly healing my brokenness, of truly leaning into the glory of a story that was not always pretty but is truly what made me who I am today.

So, as you sit here at the beginning of your journey through this delightful book, I want you to know how very proud I am of you for being brave enough to turn another page, to look both backward and forward, and to redefine love for yourself.

I hope your journey is filled with breakthroughs and grace and that, after reading and practicing as Sara suggests, your life is as singularly beautiful as Sara's. She did not step from bad to better. She did not step from pretending it was okay to everything being wonderful. She took intentional action and found—as I hope you do through this wonderful book—a safe place to rest.

-Karen Grosz
Author of *Quiet Leadership* and *What's Next*
and founder of Canvas Creek Team Building

PROLOGUE

"Your vision will become clear only when you can look into your own heart. Who looks outside, dreams; who looks inside, awakes."

Carl Jung

How I got here.

I GREW UP IN A FAMILY THAT WAS PUBLICLY perfect and privately shattered. We were big fish in a very small sea (more of a pond, really) in rural Montana.

I hopped the first bus out of town after high school. That bus was in the form of an equally shattered person. We were both just eighteen. We spent twelve and a half years together, eight and a half of those married, none of them happy.

We were miserable, but boy did we look good. My husband and I earned lots of scholarships and degrees. We smiled in photos. We dressed well. I had excellent highlights.

All that posturing was exhausting. At the end of every day, I had nothing left to just be me. I understand now that all I really wanted was to be accepted (i.e., *loved*) by my family of origin. My marriage had nothing to do with the person I married. Neither of us had the slightest notion of what love really is.

Being "perfect" was the only thing I'd ever known.

It was my heritage, a family tradition. I didn't realize I wasn't being myself until the façade finally crumbled when I was thirty-one. Seemingly overnight, I was a highly educated, unemployed single mom with a toddler son and almost nothing else. No flashy husband. No new house. No impressive job. No sense of self.

And that was when life got good. That was when I slowly redefined love. It took nine years. Nine long, hard years of therapy, research, prayer, study, wash, rinse, repeat.

It took courage. I didn't know I had to use a voice I'd never even heard before. (Neither had anybody else, and a lot of people didn't much like the sound of it and still don't!)

Not coincidentally, it was during these years that I fell in love—first with my son, then with my amazing friends, then with a man, then (finally!) with myself. It would have been far easier if I'd learned to love myself first, but I hadn't yet redefined love.

My circle has now grown to include another son and the most incredible self-made family a person could ask for. My circle grows bigger every day. I am blessed beyond measure.

I am still a work in progress. I have so much more love to give. When I started this journey, I wasn't an expert. I was just someone who got tired of living a lie—the lie that love is always happy, warm, and tender.

There are always going to be people who are harder to love than others. For me, it is those who have hurt me, who continue to attempt to hurt me, and who refuse to take any accountability.

But I forge ahead, loving myself and others through it. Love may not be the only emotion that I feel when I encounter these people. I have a finely tuned death stare that still rears its ugly head.

We all have complicated relationships, and I am certainly no exception. It is these very relationships that have brought me to this place, and for that I am grateful. I am as imperfect as anyone else. I have been known to hurt others during my journey towards healing. If you're not willing to admit your fallibility and mistakes, then you cannot redefine love.

My journey began when I wanted to give my son something different from the life I'd known. Then I realized I wanted something different for myself. And thus began the quest of a lifetime—the journey to the center of myself.

I sought therapy. I read books and articles. I reached out to others who'd had similar experiences. And I spent a lot of time online, searching. What was I searching for? From every resource, I was seeking the same things—validation, encouragement, permission.

Permission for what?

I didn't know at the time. In hindsight, I know I wanted permission to redefine love. I wanted permission to say "Enough!" to those who hurt me but to still love them at the same time.

There is a lot of information out there about love and forgiveness. And there is a lot of information about setting boundaries. But too often, the resources for dysfunctional families and broken relationships address one or the other—fight (stand up for yourself) or flight (forgive and forget or leave those jerks behind).

I wanted a place to go that gave me permission to take care of myself without fear, without fight, flight, or freeze.

I was tired of fighting and falling back, fighting and falling back. My entire life had been spent endlessly battling and retreating with no rest. I was physically and emotionally exhausted.

I hope *Redefining Love* gives you what I couldn't find—a safe place to rest. You don't have to fight or fall back. You can stand your ground without anger. You can set firm boundaries and tell hard truths with love. It's okay to have it both ways. In fact, it's essential that you do.

We live in a culture where everything is politicized, even love. But it doesn't have to be that way. My life experience has provided me with the unique opportunity to live and love people from all walks of American life. I've split my adulthood between two states—one red, one blue—and there are things I love about each of them.

Regardless of your politics, your religion, your income, or background, rural or urban, we all have an equal capacity for good and evil and an infinite ability to love.

I imagine a time when enough of us have mastered redefining love that we can be at peace with everyone, regardless of our differences. I imagine a time when we are fully at peace with ourselves. Our culture isn't there yet, but each time someone heals from trauma, we are one step closer to healing our culture.

Who I am.

Professionally, I am a boundaries and trauma coach and the creator of the Redefining Love Framework. I have spent my career working primarily in social work and writing, with a brief stopover in accounts payable. (That's a long story for another time.)

But perhaps more importantly, I am a person on this journey with you. I am someone who has felt the sting of rejection on a massive scale, more than once. When I decided to figure out where everything went wrong in my seemingly perfect life, I poured myself into healing.

I am a recovering overthinker, overachiever, and people pleaser. I haven't figured everything out. I haven't mastered my theory. I make mistakes every day. But every day I'm growing, learning, and helping as many people as I can to heal.

This book provides a foundation for the Redefining Love Framework. I anticipate this will be an evolving work, with many editions as my life, career, and experience provides fresh insights into ever-broader ways to guide others through boundaries, accountability, and grace.

Redefining Love offers a roadmap to inform your journey through even your deepest hurts and disappointments. It doesn't matter where you start; what matters is simply that you begin.

I hope my ideas inspire you, and I hope you will reach out for help from a healthy support system if you need it. There is never any shame in seeking help. If you feel alone, unloved, or unworthy, reach out. There is love out there for you! Keep seeking it until you find what you need to feel emotionally safe to grow.

CRUCIAL NOTE:

If you are experiencing physical or sexual abuse, setting personal boundaries for yourself *is not enough*! You need help. Physical or sexual violence is *not* because you haven't set clear boundaries. In fact, it has nothing to do with you and everything to do with the abuser's need for power and control. Reach out to someone you trust and keep speaking out until you are heard and *safe*.

PART ONE
An Introduction to Redefining Love

ONE

A New Definition of Love

"Love yourself first, and everything else falls into line. You really have to love yourself to get anything done in this world."

Lucille Ball

REDEFINING LOVE IS NOT JUST ABOUT ROMANTIC love. It's about how we relate to *everyone* around us, from casual acquaintances to our friendships, our children, our families of origin, and yes, our romantic partners.

Redefining Love is *not* a trauma healing modality. It is a foundational mindset framework that allows space for our own mental health within high conflict relationships. If we haven't allowed space for ourselves, the trauma-healing modalities aren't going to help.

So many times, I've heard people say that "therapy just doesn't work for me." Their lack of success in therapy becomes another source of shame that adds to their general sense of failure at life.

Some people go "healing hopping," bouncing from one modality to the next. Talk therapy, acupuncture, breathwork, reiki, art therapy, yoga... you name it, they've tried it. They leave these sessions with a sense of relief and release, yet they always end up slipping back into old, dysfunctional patterns.

The problem isn't in the modalities. I've seen enormous healing take place through many different healing techniques. It's true that there is no one-size-fits-all magic modality that works for everyone. Sometimes, we need to try out different options to find the one that best suits our unique temperament and experiences.

But, if an individual has tried them all and nothing has worked, it may be that they are missing important elements that typically are not a part of most healing modalities. When an individual is experiencing shame, guilt, and a sense of shame related to "failure" at therapy, it's time to explore that gap between the therapy and the healing that they seek. Otherwise, the time and money invested in healing goes to waste, and they may even be making circumstances worse by piling on additional shame due to their lack of success in therapy.

Based on my observations of the healing journeys of others, as well as my own, I discovered three key ingredients necessary for the benefits of a healing modality to "stick" beyond the initial post-session high. Those individuals who were able to integrate lasting change had healthy *boundaries*, appropriate *accountability*, and a whole lot of *grace*.

When there is a shortage of boundaries, accountability, and grace, the healing doesn't integrate into our day-to-day lives. That moment of sharing or meditation or healing touch feels like a release. It's liberating in the moment, but when we go back into our lives where nobody else in our circle is doing the same healing work, the dysfunction picks up where it left off. When we get back into the real world, outside of that safe therapeutic space, we fall right back into the same patterns.

The problem lies in the fact that despite our best efforts at healing, we still have the same complicated relationships. We still have the same power struggles, hurts, and disappointments. And very often, we have no idea how to extract ourselves from the shame cycles – cycles that very often started generations ago that are deeply ingrained in the structure of our families and culture.

This is where the Redefining Love Framework comes in. Redefining Love serves as a bridge between our attempts at healing our trauma and our complicated, messy real lives. Because we don't exist in a vacuum, and those we encounter as we move through our lives are not growing in the same direction or doing life in the same way.

The Redefining Love Framework is a mindset paradigm that teaches people how to set boundaries and hold themselves and others accountable with grace. The philosophy is built on a foundation of Three Pillars: Boundaries, Accountability, and Grace.

To successfully redefine love, all three of these concepts must be present. Without each of these, redefining love is not possible. Each of the Three Pillars must be applied both internally (towards yourself) and externally (towards others).

What this means is that a person must look inward and define who they are and what they stand for (boundaries), give themselves credit for their strengths and openly admit their weaknesses (accountability), and love themselves through their pain, disappointment, and heartache (grace).

These same principles can be applied externally as well. This manifests as boundaries in the way they are traditionally applied with self-advocacy, but also by respecting others' boundaries as applied to you. In doing so, you hold others accountable for their words and actions, and you can do all these with love and understanding that most people are doing the best they can with the temperament and experiences they've been given, which is grace.

Let's talk about love...

We are social creatures. We know instinctively that we need love to survive. Even the most independent people are hungry for love. Not only do we need to receive it, but we also need to give it to be fully human.

Webster's defines love this way: 1) strong affection for another arising out of kinship or personal ties, and 2) attraction based on sexual desire; affection and tenderness felt by lovers.[1]

Love is associated with feelings of warm regard, mutual respect, and admiration. Love is a positive thing, right?

Certainly, it is. Until it's not.

I was a social worker for many years. I saw a lot of brokenness and pain. I saw parents betray children at monumental levels. And yet, the children in these situations *always* loved their parents, regardless of how badly they'd been hurt by them.

Why is that? Because we are programmed to love. It is literally written into our genetic code.[2] We are born vulnerable and dependent. *Love* is what connects us so that we rely on others, so that we can take care of others, so that humanity can survive.

It is *love* that drives children to run away from (safe) foster homes back to a neglectful, drug-addicted parent. In many cases, when someone hurts us, it is because we *love* them. If we didn't, we wouldn't care so much about their actions.

When we are emotionally hurt, we are called *heartbroken*. Literally, we are raised from infancy with the idea that if love doesn't feel good, we are *broken*.

And since in reality nothing can *always* be good 100 percent of the time, there is not a single person among us who reaches adulthood without some measure of brokenness. Even the most sheltered child is disappointed by those they love from time to time.

When isn't it love?

Love, as it is defined by culture, can sometimes motivate us to make poor choices. We've all hurt someone we love at one point or another. We say something hurtful out of anger. We forget an occasion that is very important to someone else. We get so caught up in our fears and insecurities that we don't think about how our actions impact others. These things are simply part of the human experience.

However, love *never* motivates us to betray others, to physically harm others, to threaten others, or to control others. That is a need for *power,* not love. And although an abuse survivor may stay in an abusive romantic relationship due in part to love, it also very likely involves financial dependence, child custody, and a debilitating sense of shame and self-loathing.

Betrayal, control, and abuse—emotional, physical, sexual, or spiritual—is the opposite of love.

It can be hard to recognize the difference between power and love, particularly in relationships where there is established authority, such as parenting and complementarian romantic relationships. When we experience heartbreak, our ability to be objective is diminished.

At the core of all heartbreak is fear.

We fear being alone. We fear being worthless. Fear triggers a primal fight, flight, freeze, or fawn response[3], and *whoosh!* Rationality flies right out the window, right along with our self-worth.

It took me forty years of heartbreak and hours of therapy to realize that it doesn't have to be this way. I'm not broken. I'm fully human, with a full and deep capacity for love.

Before I could get to this point, I had to completely rework my concept of love. I have come to the conclusion that Webster's has it wrong. (Sorry, Webster's.) Love is not *always* strong affection and attraction.

As I traversed through my trauma-healing journey, I came up with an alternative definition of love that has served me far better:

Love is an act of courage. Love is facing fear of rejection and worthlessness head-on.

Love is knowing who we are, and being true to that, regardless of what others think.

Love is accepting ourselves and others where we are at, even if that isn't a very pleasant place.

Love is *honest,* even when it hurts. And sometimes, love means walking away from relationships or habits that are not serving a positive purpose in our life.

If love is always honest, then we can't tiptoe around our pain. We must face it head-on. We must speak up when we are wronged, and we must admit when we have wronged others. This requires three things: boundaries, accountability, and grace.

Without these key ingredients, we might feel affection and attraction, but we do not have love.

Once I redefined love, my world blew wide open.

I felt safe to say *NO.* I knew where I ended and others began. I stopped running from myself and for the first time realized that I had beautiful gifts to share with the world.

I no longer had to choose between loving someone and my emotional or physical well-being.

I no longer had to swear off all affection for people I disagreed with. (Phew, couldn't we *all* do without that these days?)

The Redefining Love Framework allowed me to love those who hurt, disappointed, and even disgusted me from a safe distance.

I'd always struggled with the idea of grace.

Why should I offer love to those who are cruel to me or others? This new definition of love allowed me to love people despite their shortcomings. Love no longer required adoration or warm affection. It only required honesty, accountability for myself and others, boundaries, and grace.

Redefining love is *universal.* We aren't meant to love only those we hold in warm regard. We must love *everyone,* but we get to choose where each individual fits into our life, if at all. (Later on, we'll learn that love doesn't provide a "free jerk pass.")

Redefining love creates space to choose with whom you'll share your time. When we are faced with toxic relationships, we don't have to deem the individual unworthy of love. We must simply love them from a *safe distance.*

We are culturalized to believe that love is always happy.

If love is *always* warm, if it is *always* nurturing, then when someone we love makes us feel sad, angry, disappointed, or disgusted, we become disoriented. When those we love hurt us, we become afraid.

If love is equal to trust and adoration, and we don't always feel positive about our love relationships, does this mean we are bad at giving or receiving love? Does this mean we are unlovable or incapable of loving others?

We are afraid of those who are different from us. If love is always a warm feeling of affection, then loving someone we strongly disagree with or dislike is an impossibility. All this confusion creates fear, which breeds loneliness, bitterness, spite, rage, and darkness.

This is the state I found myself in when I began my journey through my trauma. I was terrified of trusting others, and every time I did, I was disappointed. People kept screwing up, and I kept getting hurt.

My definition of love did not allow for mistakes, pain, or selfishness. I did not know how to give myself or others grace. I felt like the only option was to lock up my heart and hide it in lonely isolation.

Once I redefined love, after a lifetime of living in a perpetual state of fight, flight, or freeze, I could *finally* relax.

For the first time in forty years, I understood what happiness felt like.

I could forgive even the deepest hurts.

I could open myself up to new and lasting relationships.

I could trust myself to make healthy connections with others.

And I could set boundaries with love.

If you've made it this far into the book, I've probably got you interested in the Redefining Love Framework. If you are tired of feeling angry, resentful, hurt, and blown off course by what feels like uncontrollable circumstances, you are reading the right book.

It can feel scary to step into the unknown, and sometimes I'm going to ask you to be *brave*. But you *can* do it! And I promise; it is so worth it.

Two

How Do I Redefine Love?

"Start where you are.
Use what you have.
Do what you can."

Arthur Ashe

REDEFINING LOVE STARTS WHEREVER YOU ARE. There is no starting line or ribbon to burst through at the end. There is only your journey inward and outward, all at once.

It feels like a paradox—before we can effectively love others, we must love ourselves. Before we can love ourselves, we must love others. Fortunately, the opposite is also true.

Once you love others despite your disagreements and conflicts, you start to love yourself as well. Once you start loving yourself, it becomes so much easier to love others. And once you get the hang of it, it *all* works together for your good.

It truly doesn't matter where you start. But for our purposes—for the sake of instruction—let's choose a starting point.

Let's start with YOU.

It seems as good a place as any, right? Wouldn't you like to make peace with regret and forgive yourself for your mistakes? Wouldn't it be nice to let go of shame and self-doubt?

Doing all these things requires that you be honest and accountable, not only about your shortcomings and failures but also about your successes. In my experience, it is often harder for a person to honestly account for their strengths than their weaknesses.

DIVERSION…

Why is that, anyway? Put the book down and think for a moment. Do you find it easier to list your strengths or your weaknesses?

If you are someone who struggles with the idea of self-love, you may be confused about what self-love looks like. Self-love is *not* conceit, narcissism, or self-absorption. Narcissists don't love *anyone* in a healthy way, including themselves. Redefining love requires accountability, which is impossible for the self-absorbed.

The facts of love:

To redefine love, there are some basic facts about love that you must accept that will likely challenge your current concept of what love is:

1. *Love is messy.* Love is not always the way it is portrayed in our culture and the media. Love isn't always warm and fuzzy. And it certainly isn't always easy. Families, romances, children, friends, coworkers,

perfect strangers… relationships are complicated and untidy. (And, as we'll learn later, you can't have any kind of relationship without love.)

2. *We are all a blessing and a curse.* We are all flawed and ugly at times, capable of incredible light and despicable dark. Yes, you, too. That's where accountability comes in. Until you can accept that we all have good *and* evil within us, you are never going to be able to redefine love.

Most of us tend to fall somewhere on the spectrum between believing that all people are basically good or believing all people are basically selfish. One way or another, most of us need to realize that people are made of equal parts of both.

Seeing the darkness in those we love can be difficult. Seeing it in ourselves can be almost impossible. And if you are a self-loather like I was, seeing your light may be equally difficult.

SUPER HELPFUL TIP!

I will emphasize over and over throughout this book the benefits of therapy. If you are having trouble holding others or yourself accountable (good or bad), I strongly recommend you seek out professional help. I am not at all ashamed to admit that there is no way I could have made it to where I am today without the help of a professional therapist.

3. *Relationship.* What does it mean to be in *relationship* with someone else? In *Redefining Love*, relationship equals interaction. Every time you participate in social media or step out of your house, you are in relationship with others. We are in relationship with *everyone*.

If I am in relationship with everyone, then everyone deserves equal regard. The clerk at the grocery store is just as deserving of love from me as my husband and children.

And since we get to decide at what distance we love someone, I get to decide how I will express that love. Will I look them in the eye? Ask how their day is going? Say thank you after they ring up my purchase? That seems easy enough, right?

But what about the guy on the news in the white hood burning a cross? Or an abusive parent? A conniving coworker? Or the kid who bullies your kid at school? Suddenly, the idea of loving everyone gets a lot harder. But just because something is hard, it doesn't mean it is a worthwhile endeavor.

We must nurture our relationships with love for those relationships to function properly. And we are in relationship with *everyone* because, in one way or another, each of us affects the whole. (Suddenly, you can see how *Redefining Love* has the potential to change the world, one individual at a time.)

And before you start feeling overwhelmed by the idea of loving the whole world, keep in mind that each relationship within the whole is unique, and you get to determine with boundaries how close you want each relationship to be. Your capacity for love is infinite. Your time and energy are *not*.

The Three Pillars

There is no step-by-step path to redefining love. As mentioned in Chapter 1, the Redefining Love Framework is built on the Three Pillars of Boundaries, Accountability, and Grace. Without these three pillars working together, redefining love cannot be achieved.

Every relationship—and every interaction within that relationship—comes with its unique circumstances. One relationship may require you to start with grace for yourself. Another might require that you apply boundaries for another. And yet another may require accountability for both yourself and others. It doesn't matter where you start, only that you *start*.

Boundaries.

We all have a right to decide who we will allow into our inner circle. Enmeshed families and codependents will try to convince you that you are stuck with them. But the reality is, unless you are an underage minor* or physically in danger,** you are not stuck with anyone. You have a right to choose your family (more on this in Chapter 13).

*If you are an underage minor, setting boundaries can be tricky. Your legal guardians have a say in many layers of your life, and you are reliant on adults for food, shelter, and other necessities of life. You may not have the same opportunities to set boundaries as an adult, but you can still set internal boundaries and begin the work of determining what space you take up in the world.

**If you are physically unsafe, setting boundaries is not going to be enough to protect you. Someone who does not respect your body in the most basic sense of safety is not going to respect your boundaries, no matter how well you advocate for yourself. Additionally, your body and mind are going to stay in a triggered state until you are no longer in physical danger. You are in no condition to start boundaries work until you are in a safe and emotionally secure environment.

If you feel physically unsafe, please seek help. Get to a safe location, and then call the National Domestic Violence Hotline at 1(800)799-SAFE (7233) or visit thehotline.org. You will receive assistance to help you escape and rebuild your life.

A major component of the Redefining Love Framework is deciding with whom we want to share our whole selves. There is only so much of us to go around. Emotionally healthy people choose to share their whole selves only with those who respect their boundaries because their boundaries are essentially who they are. If they don't respect your boundaries, they don't respect *you*.

The idea that setting boundaries is unloving is a myth. In fact, it is quite the opposite. When someone sets a personal boundary for us, they are saying, "I love you enough to share my whole self with you." How's that for a compliment? Instead of being offended by other people's boundaries, we should feel flattered that they trust us enough to be open.

We'll talk more about Boundaries in Chapter 4.

Accountability.

Typically, accountability is the part of *Redefining Love* my coaching clients look forward to the *least*. The word "accountability" feels punitive, so much so that I considered not using it. I considered the words *intentional* and *examination*. And certainly, these two elements are required for accountability. But here's the thing…

Accountability is the only word for it. There must be some sort of *accounting* that happens—some sort of intentional examination of the motives and actions of yourself and others. Without accountability, you can't set boundaries for yourself or anyone else, and you can't give yourself and others grace if you don't know where grace needs to be given.

Holding ourselves accountable involves digging way down deep into our darkness and light and admitting where we've done wrong (and right). It's scary, and it hurts. It's also crucial because if you hold other people accountable without holding yourself to the same standard, you become sanctimonious.

I will say it again—counseling is highly recommended, particularly if you are a product of a dysfunctional family. The primary characteristic of dysfunction is a lack of accountability. If you grew up in a toxic household, you were provided little to no foundation to build upon and no tools with which to mine within yourself.

Holding others accountable can also be scary. When we call others out on their bad behavior, even when it's done gently and with the best of intentions, we risk rejection. We risk conflict. We risk anger and hurt feelings. At the very least, it's uncomfortable.

It's much easier to just keep your mouth shut, right? Maybe. But it isn't honest. Sometimes silence is the biggest lie of all. And it certainly isn't loving. How can anyone hope to grow and become their best self if nobody ever points out their areas for improvement?

The belief that we are in relationship with *everyone* holds everyone accountable. No one exists in a vacuum. The actions of one person *always* affect someone else, which affects someone else, which affects someone else. There is power in relationship when we realize that we are all truly connected. And with great power comes great responsibility (or so says Uncle Ben to Spiderman).

We will talk more about Accountability in Chapter 5.

The Shame Cycle.

When I am working on loving those in my personal life who deeply hurt me, I am tempted to get defensive. This defensiveness is the root of gossip and drama. We drag other people into our pain to vindicate ourselves and validate our feelings. We become hurt not only by the person who committed the offense against us but also by all those who side with the other person. Battle lines are drawn, and fight or flight is in full swing.

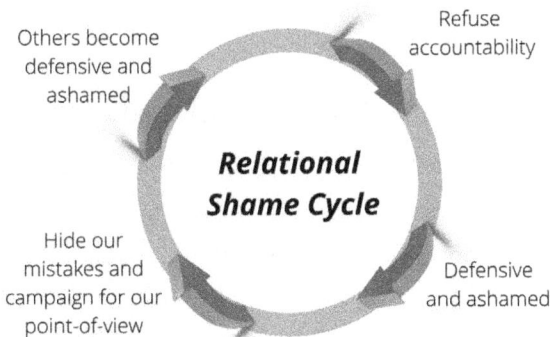

Others become defensive and ashamed

Refuse accountability

Relational Shame Cycle

Defensive and ashamed

Hide our mistakes and campaign for our point-of-view

SARA BETH WALD

This is when it becomes crucial that we see the equal capacity for good and evil in ourselves and others. When we have accepted that each one of us has light and dark within us, we can recognize that a person may be a blessing to one and a curse to another. We can then allow others their journey. We can accept blessings from someone who has hurt others (as we all have) and allow others to appreciate the blessings offered by those who have hurt us.

We will talk more about the Shame Cycle in Chapter 10.

Grace.

The only way to end a shame cycle is to apply grace. Grace simply means allowing yourself and someone else their journey. Grace is where self-love and other-love come into play.

Grace happens when you look at the good intentions behind a mistake, and you see all the ways that culture, upbringing, experiences, and temperament come into play. Grace leads to forgiving yourself and others. Without grace, accountability for self leads to self-loathing, and accountability for others leads to self-righteousness. And so, grace is crucial to redefining love.

We will talk more about Grace in Chapter 6.

When Redefining Love is achieved.

Once we have redefined love, setting boundaries and holding others accountable becomes a lot less scary. Even though the other person may still not see it that way, within yourself you know that you are sharing your whole, honest self with the other person. And you don't have to be angry or aggressive about it because you are sharing an act of love.

There are always going to be people who are harder to love than others. For me, it is those who have hurt me, who continue to attempt to hurt me, and who refuse any accountability. For others, it may be those with completely different worldviews. (Politics and love aren't generally terms we use in the same breath.)

But we must forge ahead, loving ourselves and others through it. Love may not be the first emotion that you feel when you encounter these people. Sometimes it may take days to come to a place of love for someone else. But it is so incredibly worth it. Because love feels a lot better than hate, bitterness, and despair.

I imagine a world where everyone has redefined love, a world where everyone holds themselves and others accountable, where everyone holds firm to their boundaries, and everyone else respects those boundaries because they recognize it as an act of love.

I imagine a world where we can all love through our disagreements, where we realize that each of us has good and evil within us, that each of us is both a blessing and a curse. The world I imagine isn't perfect. We are all still flawed. We all make mistakes that hurt others. The only real difference is we love each other anyway.

The way we view love really is just cultural. And culture can be changed, one individual at a time. And so, it begins right where it started. With *you*.

PART TWO
THE THREE PILLARS

THREE

THE THREE PILLARS

"A house must be built on solid foundations if it is to last. The same principle applies to man, otherwise he too will sink back into the soft ground and become swallowed up by the world of illusion."

Sai Baba

REDEFINING LOVE IS BUILT ON A FOUNDATION of Three Pillars: Boundaries, Accountability, and Grace. To achieve redefined love, you must maintain a balance between the Three Pillars, not only for others but also for yourself.

Here's a graphic that illustrates how the Three Pillars work together for a balanced life:

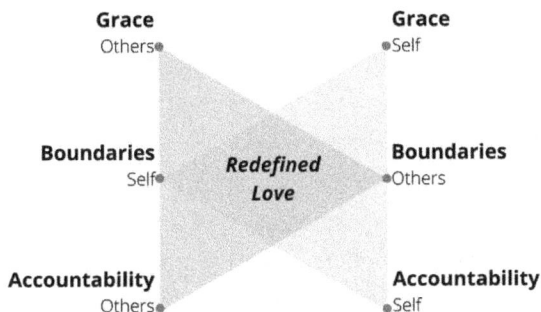

Let's define each of these terms:

Boundaries:

Boundaries for Self: Boundaries determine where you end and other people begin. Without boundaries, there is no you. To love yourself, you must know who you are. In order to know who you are, you must establish boundaries. You must clearly define the space you occupy in the world, and you must give yourself permission to reside in that space.

Boundaries for Others: Setting boundaries is so much more than simply telling people no occasionally. When you set a boundary with someone, you are establishing a protective barrier between yourself and the other person, to whatever degree is necessary, for your mental and emotional well-being.

An Act of Love: When we set a boundary with someone else, we are showing them that we love them enough to tell them who we really are. When we redefine love, we can love people despite our differences, even if they hurt us.

Some people must be loved from a safe distance.

That distance may be physical, social, or emotional. Maybe we choose not to socialize with them anymore, but we continue to maintain the same activities, church, or community. This type of boundary really doesn't affect our day-to-day routine. It just means that you decide this person isn't going to be a part of your close social network.

Maybe we choose not to share our deepest thoughts and feelings with them, or our successes and failures. This type of boundary works well for family members or coworkers we must continue to interact with. Just because we see them frequently doesn't mean we have to allow them into our close circle of support.

And maybe, if the person is truly dangerous or highly emotionally toxic, we choose to distance ourselves physically from them or limit interactions to only public places.

Accountability:

Accountability for Self: You are not a victim of your emotions. You are the boss of your feelings. You are not a victim of circumstantial relationships. You can choose where you end and others begin and with whom you want to share your life.

Accountability for Others: When we redefine love, we recognize that we can love people through anger, hurt, and disagreements. And we realize that ignoring the weaknesses in ourselves and others is a far greater betrayal than being honest about our feelings and experiences.

Grace:

Grace for Self: Grace is the self-respect we feel despite our flaws. It is the key to self-forgiveness (and forgiveness in general). Grace is the guidepost of the gate we can choose to hold open or respectfully close, depending on how others fit into our personal voyage through life.

Grace for Others: Grace is the love we hold for everyone, despite our differences. It is the ability to look at someone's shortcomings with compassion and empathy. Grace is the peace we find when we allow others their path. Grace allows us to view conflict not as a negative to be avoided but as an opportunity to better understand another person. Perhaps we have something to learn from them or they from us.

Once we have redefined love to allow for the messy, painful aspects of the human experience, we can love everyone, regardless of their beliefs. We don't have to take sides because love is not determined by whether someone makes us feel warmth and affection. Grace allows us to set boundaries and, sometimes, love people from a distance.

Grace is the willingness to accept that we all view the world through the lens of our experiences.

FOUR

BOUNDARIES

*"We need to have a talk on the subject of what's
yours and what's mine."*

Steig Larsson

BOUNDARIES DETERMINE WHERE YOU END AND
other people begin. In enmeshed family systems or codependent relationships, there are few, if any, boundaries. Without
boundaries, there is no you.

To love yourself, you must know who you are. In order
to know who you are, you must establish boundaries. You
must clearly define the space you occupy in the world, and
you must give yourself permission to reside in that space.

Setting boundaries is so much more than simply saying
no occasionally. Setting boundaries involves digging deep
to identify who you are and what you believe in and then
establishing a protective barrier between yourself and others
to the degree you feel necessary for your mental and emotional well-being.

This means that while you allow certain people in—say,
your spouse or your children, or closest friends—you may
keep others at a further distance.

It is important to note that boundaries can evolve and change for the same person over the course of a lifetime. When a child becomes an adult, the boundaries between parent and child must adapt for the relationship to remain healthy. If you go through a divorce, the way you relate to your former spouse needs to become entirely different than it was when you were married.

If one or both parties are unwilling to change the dynamics of the relationship, the relationship will become strained and possibly break. If you've never been divorced, this may seem like a strange thing to say. Isn't the relationship already broken? Well, yes, the marriage relationship is over. But unless you are childless, one or both of you change all your friends and social connections, and you move across the country from one another, you will still have a relationship. It won't be a marriage anymore, but you will have to figure out a new way of relating to each other.

To maintain healthy connections, we must be willing to adapt our boundaries as our circumstances change. And we must seek out close relationships with those who approach boundaries like we do .

To redefine love, you must truly and deeply love yourself. You must realize that you have as much right to take up space in the world as anybody else. You must draw a link around that space and determine for yourself who you will allow into your life and to what degree.

How do I set boundaries?

Speaking from experience, if you are a person who has struggled to set limits in the past, or you aren't even sure who you are and where you fit into the world, it can feel overwhelming to suddenly begin setting boundaries.

The good news is that you don't need to start having big confrontations with everyone around you to set healthy boundaries. In fact, if big confrontations are required for your boundaries to be taken seriously, it may be time to reexamine whether this is a healthy relationship for you to maintain and to what level.

Just as there is no step-by-step guide to redefining love, there is no step-by-step guide to setting boundaries. But don't let that overwhelm you. In fact, let it free you to start exactly where you're at, regardless of where that may be.

Here are some actions you can take as you begin your boundaries journey.

Focus on what's going on for you internally.

How do you talk to yourself? How often do you feel like banging your head against a wall and saying, "Stupid! Stupid! Stupid!" after someone has gotten the best of you? How often, once again, have you said yes when you wanted to say no, or you didn't speak up when you wish you had? Can you laugh at your mistakes, or do you beat yourself up about every little misstep?

You might be wondering what talking to yourself has to do with boundaries. In truth, it has *everything* to do with boundaries. Why? Because if you don't love yourself enough to talk kindly to yourself, how on earth are you ever going to love yourself enough to expect others to respect you and the space you take up in the world?

Those of us who came of age in the '90s watching *Saturday Night Live* are familiar with a character named Stuart Smalley, brought to life by comedian Al Franken (before he became a politician). The gist of the sketch was that Stuart was a therapist who encouraged his clients to talk to themselves in the mirror to develop self-love.

Sometimes he'd talk to himself, and other times he'd have a pretend counseling session with the guest host—usually some giant celebrity who presumably had a healthy self-image, such as Michael Jordan or Kevin Bacon. He'd face them towards the mirror and ask them to repeat the phrases, "I'm good enough. I'm smart enough, and doggone it, people like me."

It was funny because we assume that the people saying these phrases were already aware that they were good enough, smart enough, and that people liked them. (Then again, maybe not. How often have you assumed someone else "had it all" only to watch them fall apart?)

The Stuart Smalley bit was just comedy. But there is some good advice there. Before others can respect you and your boundaries, you must treat *yourself* with respect. This means you need to dig deep and get honest about how you're talking to yourself.

Here's a great exercise. The next time you are beating yourself up about something, imagine that your best friend did whatever it was you are feeling crummy about. How would you respond to them? I'm guessing you wouldn't call them stupid, or get angry and frustrated, or slap their forehead. So why are you doing that to yourself? Don't you deserve just as much respect as the next person?

Be your own best friend. When you feel yourself slipping into self-abuse, remember that you are good enough, smart enough, and gosh darn it, people like you!

Take mental notes.

If you are new to setting boundaries, you probably have gotten good at ignoring your discomfort cues. To survive, you've disregarded your feelings to accommodate those around you.

Stop doing this! If something makes you uncomfortable, let yourself think about it. Sit in that discomfort for a little while. Figure out what about the interaction makes you uncomfortable. Do the person's words feel hurtful? Do you feel as though they don't respect your time and/or space?

Let's talk about triggers here for a bit. Triggers are things that illicit a strong negative emotional response. We all have triggers. They aren't something to be ashamed of. But we do need to be aware of them. Not only are they important for accountability—because, left unchecked, our triggers can bring out the worst in us—but it's also important to distinguish between actual boundary violations and our personal triggers.

Just because someone really ticks us off doesn't necessarily mean they are violating our boundaries. It may be that they are simply doing something that trips one of our triggers. To properly set boundaries, you have to be aware of your triggers.

As you can see, proper boundary setting requires a lot of introspection, which is part of personal accountability. From this, perhaps you're beginning to understand how each of the Three Pillars is necessary to redefine love.

Start small.

Once you've learned to identify your discomfort cues, it's time to take the leap into boundary setting. This can feel scary and uncomfortable at first. That's totally normal. Most people who struggle with setting boundaries have been that way their entire lives and probably had their lack of boundaries reinforced by unhealthy family, friend, and romantic relationships.

I recommend taking baby steps. Give yourself lots of grace. At the beginning of your boundary journey, you're going to fall back into old patterns at first. And, if you're anything like me, your first attempts at setting boundaries are going to be defensive, angry, and/or timid. It's all okay. You must start somewhere.

Imagine it like learning to play the piano. Children who are taught from a very young age can pick up instruments much easier than an adult who had little exposure to music. It wouldn't be fair to expect an adult with no musical experience to sit down at a piano and play Beethoven.

Similarly, if you have reached adulthood with little or no experience with boundaries, it is unreasonable to expect yourself to be an immediate expert. Start with something simple. Do you secretly hate hugs? Figure out a way to communicate this to others in a good-natured way. Be honest. Smile and say, "No thanks. I'm not a hugger."

Are you always the person the PTA, church, and fundraisers call because they know you'll say yes, even if you are frequently overwhelmed? The next time someone asks you to volunteer, and you get that sinking feeling in your gut, take a deep breath, smile, and say, "I'd love to help, but I just have too much going on right now."

Does this mean you'll never be drawn into an awkward hug again? Or never get in over your head with volunteering? (Or whatever boundary you decide to start with.) Of course not. When it happens, don't beat yourself up because you didn't maintain your boundaries. Just love yourself through it, learn from it, and move on.

Whatever you choose to start with, make sure it's reasonable. For most of us, especially those who grew up in enmeshed family systems or have spent a long time in codependent relationships, setting boundaries feels downright scary.

Simply telling a pushy coworker you need to stop chatting so you can focus on your work makes you sweat! This is your fight, flight, or freeze response being triggered because you believe that any conflict is negative and all boundaries are mean. So, let's talk about that…

Reframe the picture.

Let me clear the air here. You're not mean because you set boundaries. In fact, setting boundaries is very kind. Wouldn't you rather know how someone else is feeling and who someone is than wonder where you stand?

The only people who don't like boundaries are people who aren't interested in truly, fully knowing you. For whatever reason, they consider your autonomy as a person a threat (and the reason probably has nothing to do with you and everything to do with generational trauma). Are these people with whom you want to be in close relationship?

A major part of *Redefining Love* is deciding with whom we want to share our whole selves. There is only so much of us to go around. Emotionally healthy people choose to share their whole selves with those who respect their boundaries because their boundaries reflect who they are.

You must accept the premise that if someone doesn't respect your boundaries, then they don't respect you. It really is that simple.

Setting boundaries is an act of love.

Most people know that it's important for children to be told no occasionally. Since I believe that we are all growing until the day we die, we can all benefit from ongoing "parenting" from others. We are essentially all the village raising each other.

Once we have redefined love, setting boundaries becomes a lot less scary. Even though the other person may still not see it that way, within yourself you know that you are sharing your whole, honest self with the other person. And you don't have to be angry, defensive, or aggressive about it because you are sharing an act of love.

Suddenly, telling your enmeshed family members that you are unable to attend an annual reunion becomes less scary. You love your family enough to be honest about your time availability and need for personal space, and you love yourself enough to take care of your needs.

For those of us in deeply enmeshed families and codependent relationships, it can feel very foreign to establish where we end and other people begin. If you are still having trouble figuring out what your boundaries should be, here's a list of the 20 Permissions of *Redefining Love* and the 20 Responsibilities of *Redefining Love*. Used together, these two lists become a powerful tool of introspection to help you establish the space you take up in the world.

The 20 Permissions of Redefining Love:
It's okay to feel safe.
It's okay to be different.
It's okay to create your identity.
It's okay to say no.
It's okay to fail.
It's okay to succeed.
It's okay to speak up.
It's okay to feel proud of your accomplishments.
It's okay to be separate from those you love.
It's okay to prioritize your well-being.
It's okay to refuse to keep secrets.
It's okay to walk away from drama.
It's okay to love others outside of your life partner and/or your family of origin.

It's okay to have feelings.
It's okay to disagree.
It's okay to take time for yourself.
It's okay to define your personal space.
It's okay to have your own dreams and aspirations.
It's okay to have your own interests.
It's okay to love yourself.

**The 20 Responsibilities of Redefining Love:
You have a responsibility to...**
Accept your darkness.
Accept your light.
Own your mistakes.
Say you're sorry when it's warranted.
Refuse to apologize for other people's mistakes.
Be firm but kind.
Attempt to see things from the other person's point of view.
Get emotionally and physically healthy.
Listen to reason.
Keep yourself and your children emotionally and physically safe.
Distinguish where you end and other people begin.
Set healthy boundaries.
Maintain your boundaries, even when it's uncomfortable.
Build a support system.
Educate yourself before forming an opinion.
Invest in healing.
Commit to the truth.
Be your own advocate.
Be your own best friend.
Love first.

CRUCIAL NOTE

If you are experiencing physical or sexual abuse, simply set-ting personal boundaries for yourself *is not enough*! You need help. Physical or sexual violence is *not* because you haven't set clear boundaries. In fact, it has nothing to do with you and everything to do with the abuser's need for power and control. Reach out to someone you trust and keep speaking out until you are heard and *safe*.

FIVE

ACCOUNTABILITY

"An ignorant person is inclined to blame others for his own misfortune. To blame oneself is proof of progress. But the wise man never has to blame another or himself."

Epictetus

PERHAPS THE MOST CHALLENGING PART OF redefining love is accountability. Too often, we see ourselves as victims of circumstance, swept up in relationships that spin beyond our control by some invisible force over which we have no control. This is a lie we tell ourselves to avoid accountability, and we've all done it. It's okay if you're still actively doing this. It's never too late to change your point of view.

To redefine love, you must accept the reality of choice. If someone is hurting you,* or you are hurting someone else, it's time to make a change.

*CRUCIAL NOTE:

Physical or sexual violence is *never your fault*. In fact, it has nothing to do with you and everything to do with the abuser's need for power and control. There is a myriad of ways abusers control their victims, and no amount of personal accountability or boundaries on your part is going to change that. If you are being abused, reach out to someone you trust, and keep speaking out until you are heard and *safe*.

Redefining the enemy.

We are all a mix of strengths and weaknesses, light and darkness. In *Redefining Love*, it is crucial that we see the equal capacity for good and evil in ourselves and others. When we have accepted that each one of us has within us light and darkness, we can recognize that a person may be a blessing to one and a curse to another.

We can then allow others their journeys, which is grace— one of the Three Pillars of *Redefining Love*. We can accept blessings from someone who has hurt others (as we all have) and allow others to appreciate the blessings offered by those who have hurt us.

Once we recognize that we are all capable of good and evil, we can stop assuming everyone we disagree with is our enemy. An enemy is an adversary. Enemy is a term of war, which is a place where love does not exist. If you enter conflict with other people with an attitude of winning and losing, then your focus is no longer on love but on avoiding defeat. The relationship becomes a competition for power, which shifts our focus away from accountability and towards blame.

There is no room for blame in *Redefining Love*. When we accept that we are all flawed people, we can feel compassion for ourselves and others. There is no winning or losing. There is only where you end and the other person begins. You recognize that everyone is in their own place. Perhaps that place is not somewhere you'd like to be. If that is the case, you can set healthy boundaries for yourself and shift your focus to other relationships.

Loving from a distance.

It may seem like this concept would be better placed in the Boundaries chapter. I disagree, and here's why. We can only truly love those with whom we disagree when we realize that we have as much to learn from our pain as we do from our joy. This examination is accountability, and loving from a distance is a natural result.

Therefore, to talk about loving people from a distance, we must understand accountability. This can be a scary notion because it requires us to examine our relationships with those who have hurt us, which hurts.

We must be honest with ourselves, dig deep, and root out the foundation of our hurt. We must be accountable for our healing. Keep in mind, others are responsible for their toxicity. That is theirs to carry, not yours.

Being accountable for our journey doesn't absolve the other person from their responsibilities. Let's say, for example, you were physically abused as a child. You must root out the associated shame, guilt, and self-blame that reside within you to fully love yourself and others. You must see yourself as a *survivor* rather than a victim.

Accepting responsibility for your healing doesn't mean your abuser isn't guilty of a grave offense. *Redefining Love* does not absolve others of their transgressions; it simply frees you up to love yourself and others regardless of your experiences.

In a perfect world, the other person would redefine love too, which would require that they be accountable for their actions. But we don't live in a perfect world. The only thing you can control is your healing, and your ability to redefine

41

love is not dependent upon the other person's actions one way or another.

Redefining conflict.

Most of us avoid conflict at all costs. When we call others out on their bad behavior, even when it's done gently and with love, we risk rejection. We risk anger and hurt feelings. What if the other person reacts aggressively? What if they end the relationship entirely?

It's much easier to just keep your mouth shut, right? Maybe. But it isn't honest. Sometimes silence is the biggest lie of all. And it certainly isn't loving. How can anyone hope to grow and become their best self if nobody ever points out the areas in which they need improvement?

Some people welcome conflict and even thrive on it. Our culture tends to reward these types of people, even if it is begrudgingly. We may not like bullies, but we respect them because they aren't afraid to speak up. The problem with this approach is that bullying others is just as cowardly as remaining silent. It doesn't take much courage to mistreat those who are smaller or weaker.

When someone tries to intimidate during a disagreement, their goal is to silence any dissent. And it usually works. Because most of us fear conflict, we will quietly endure intimidation because the alternative feels overwhelming. Once the dissent is silence, no progress is made to resolve the conflict.

We shy away from conflict because we see it as a negative thing, but conflict can be very constructive and is simply an unavoidable fact of life. Because the world is made up of unique individuals, each with our ideas and experiences, we aren't always going to agree.

The more we avoid conflict, the bigger the issue grows. Most of us can think of times in our lives when we avoided conflict repeatedly, until one day the issue blew up in our face. Wouldn't it have been easier to simply address it the first time the issue arose?

Accountability for self.

To break free from toxic relationships, you must first be brutally honest about your toxicity. It's okay. We all have darkness within us. It can only control you if you try to hide it from the world. The truth truly does set you free.

Even if you are an adult child of dysfunction, having had no control over the family you were born into, you have absorbed some of that toxicity into your life. If you are unwilling to address your toxicity, you will not be able to successfully redefine love.

Yes, it is humbling to admit that you've screwed up. If you have been in dysfunctional relationships, you've probably spent a lot of time blaming other people. Admitting your mistakes is even harder when nobody else is willing to admit theirs. It may feel like you're feeding yourself to the wolves. But it doesn't matter if others are being accountable or not. What matters is that you are coming to a healthier place of peace within yourself.

We have been culturalized to believe that admitting wrongdoing is akin to weakness, and weakness makes us feel ashamed. It seems easier and less painful to simply blame someone else when things don't go our way or when someone else is hurt by our actions.

Our culture has it all wrong. Holding yourself accountable is the opposite of weakness. Accountability takes enormous courage. Admitting wrongdoing and working to set things right is incredibly brave.

When we blame others for our shortcomings, we develop a victim complex. There is no greater toxicity magnet than a victim complex.

My childhood was not rosy. The adults in my world were far from perfect and were solely responsible for their behavior. But I am as flawed as anyone else. I can mourn the lost little girl I was and the way that little girl was treated. And believe me, I have. But if you are unable to move beyond your grief, it will turn to bitterness, which serves no practical purpose.

Allow yourself to feel angry about how you've been hurt. Channel that anger into courage, and then move forward with your life.

Redefining love requires you to admit your failings and account for them. I entered adulthood already deeply enmeshed in a generational shame cycle that began long before I was born. The mistreatment I endured due to other people's shame was *in no way my fault*. That doesn't absolve me of responsibility for the way my shame impacted other people (and myself).

In some of my relationships, my shame made me toxic. Notice my choice of words: *My shame* made me toxic. Not the shame of my parents, my grandparents, my siblings, or anyone else. *My shame made me toxic.* Until I was willing to address my darkness, I would continue to poison myself and others with my shame.

When I scold my children for bickering, they often respond by pointing fingers at each other. They say in unison, "He started it!" This phrase is endlessly irritating to parents. My response to them is similar to most parents: "I don't care who started it. Both of you need to *stop*."

Those I have hurt in my life were also caught in their own shame cycles and were hurting me right back. In most cases, it's impossible to even pinpoint where the toxicity began, and it doesn't matter.

I spent the majority of my twenties in a dismal state of sanctimony and self-righteousness. On the surface, I was perfect. I did not drink, do drugs, or hang out with the "wrong" people (whoever they are). I worked hard and earned the respect of my employers and colleagues.

But I wasn't perfect, and deep down I knew it. I saw bad things happening all around me and chose to remain silent. I allowed other people to define who I was and thus wasted enormous potential in myself. Rather than stand up to the bullies in my life, I bullied others who were not the true source of my angst. I wasn't blatantly evil, but my passivity was poisonous to others.

Whether you admit your shortcomings or not, you know they are there. Refusing to acknowledge your darkness makes you ashamed, which thrusts you deeper into the shame cycle.

My response to the toxic relationships in my life was to react with equal toxicity (which is so common, particularly for those of us who grew up in toxic homes—we know no other way). In therapy, I spent almost as much time discussing how I could have handled situations better than I did about the situations themselves.

I am sorry to those I've hurt. It doesn't matter how good my intentions were. It doesn't matter how justified I felt at the time. It doesn't matter how misunderstood or misconstrued I believe my actions had been.

Holding yourself accountable has nothing to do with the actions or reactions of other people. If you're not willing to admit your fallibility, you cannot redefine love.

The flip side of this, of course, is to be careful not to absorb the blame for everything wrong in your life. If you've wronged someone, own it, but do not carry the shame of others as your own.

Accountability for others.

When we care for someone deeply, it can be difficult to see their faults, especially if we accept the cultural standard of love as all or nothing. If we believe that love is *always* warm and tender, then to feel anything other than adoration means we can no longer love that person. The notion of holding people accountable is then associated with an immense sense of loss.

If the other person also views love by the cultural standard, then they may view your holding them accountable as a betrayal.

When we redefine love, we recognize that we can love people through our anger and hurt. We realize that ignoring the weakness in ourselves and others is a far greater betrayal than being honest about our feelings and experiences. We can identify where we end and the other person begins, thereby untangling ourselves from codependency and enmeshment.

Once you have learned what love truly is and what it isn't, it's easier to hold others accountable. When you redefine love, you know that there is nothing *mean* about saying, "No! Enough is enough. I deserve better in this relationship, and so do you!"

I look at it like parenting. If a child is allowed to do anything they want until their teenage years, it will be a lot harder to enforce boundaries than it would have been if the parent had reinforced appropriate behavior standards from the beginning of the child's life.

Unfortunately, many of us find ourselves stuck in toxic relationships for years before we finally realize what is happening. To be fully accountable, we must admit our place in the shame cycle.

Be careful not to fall into victim blaming. It isn't your *fault* that the other person has behaved badly. Being accountable is simply recognizing maladaptive behaviors within ourselves so that we can avoid falling into toxic relationships in the future.

Accountability is the first step to self-love. It is rooting out self-loathing and self-disgust so you can make room for loving all the wonderful things you are.

How do you determine who is accountable for what?

A healthy relationship is one in which both individuals behave with *integrity*. But what does that mean, really?

Integrity is when a person lives their life according to their values, even when it's hard or uncomfortable. And by values, I mean an intentional moral code that defines right and wrong actions, both internally (thoughts and feelings) and externally (actions).

That's a *lot* to unpack. Let's break it down by keywords:

Intentional: This means you've thought about what's important to you. You aren't just floating through life according to rules and norms passed down to you by your family, friends, coworkers, teachers, and clergy. You have a clear identity of your own that you have *intentionally* developed after careful reflection.

Moral code: These are the rules you have established for yourself based on intentional reflection. This is your sense of *right* and *wrong*. It's important to note that not everyone follows the same moral code. Our moral code is a product of culture, religion, and temperament. I talk about this more in Chapter 8.

Internal moral code: You can't live a life of integrity until you take charge of your thoughts and feelings. We all know people who look great on the outside, but when nobody's looking, they behave entirely differently.

In fact, we've all been there. To a certain extent, hypocrisy is part of the human experience. Nobody is perfect. But when hypocrisy is your go-to response to life—when your internal world and external image don't match—you are in serious misalignment. Integrity starts on the inside. You can do all the "right things" when the world is watching, but if you are a negative, toxic person inside your head, you are caught in a dangerous shame cycle that will eventually implode.

External moral code: Walk the walk, even when no one is looking. One of my favorite authors, Glennon Doyle, has mastered the art of one-sentence wisdom. One of my favorite quotes is, "Just do the next right thing."[4] Sometimes it's not black and white. Sometimes what is right is really, really hard. Or maybe what's right for you is going to disappoint someone else. That gets us to the next keyword…

Uncomfortable: Yikes. Sometimes it's hard to do the next right thing, right? Nobody ever promised you that life was going to be easy. (Or, if they did, they were pumping you full of bull.) Life is hard. Especially if you decide you're going to live your fullest, best life. Because your fullest, best life is not always going to feel warm and fuzzy. Sometimes, your best life is going to hurt. That pain is there, standing between you and all the good things. So, you must walk through it if you want to get to the other side.

Luckily, as Glennon Doyle reminds us, "We can do hard things."[5] This is perhaps her most famous and beloved quote, and there's a reason for it. We all need to be reminded of this pretty much every day. Whether you are my seven-year-old who stubbornly resisted learning to tie his shoes because it was just "too hard," or you are faced with setting boundaries with a toxic bully in your life, you *can* do hard things. Yes, you can!

Being accountable doesn't mean you're perfect.

Words like always and never are dangerous words. No matter how intentional you are, you aren't *always* going to do the right thing. Expecting yourself to *never* hurt anyone else is an unfair and unrealistic prospect. We are all different, and we are each on our own journey. Sometimes, your next right thing is going to bump up against someone else in an uncomfortable way. That's okay. It happens. The trick is to be fully present and intentional about each step and try to love yourself and the other person through it, even when it's hard.

I like to think that my husband and I have a healthy relationship. We are both focused on meeting the other's needs, openly communicating our feelings, and doing what is best for ourselves, each other, and our family.

This does *not* mean we have never hurt each other. I would love to *always* do what's right. I'd love it if my husband *never* said or did things that hurt my feelings. But that simply isn't realistic. It is an unreasonable expectation to assume that I'm never going to be hurt by those I love. It is setting up myself and my loved ones for failure.

What I *can* assume, though, is that we are all working towards the same goal—to love each other through our pain, to listen to each other when we are hurting, and to be accountable for our mistakes and shortcomings. I can safely assume this because I have chosen my relationships very carefully. I *choose* to share my life with people who are accountable for their behavior and who, in turn, hold me accountable as well.

Ideally, we would all be in healthy relationships all the time, but it isn't that simple. Sometimes we are born into toxic relationships with parents, siblings, or extended family. Sometimes we meet people who seem great at first, and it is only once we get to know them that we realize they aren't who we thought they were. And sometimes our insecurities and shame cloud our judgment and pull us into a shame cycle that we feel helpless to escape.

Toxic relationships and shame cycles may feel impossible to resolve, but that is not actually the case. I don't mean to diminish the complexity and emotional struggle it takes to extract yourself from painful relationships. Believe me; I've been there. It is not easy! But it isn't impossible.

Perhaps the hardest thing in toxic relationships is identifying *what* exactly isn't working. Usually, in these cases, you are putting a great deal of time and energy into the relationship. Often, we feel as though there just isn't anything left to give.

And perhaps you are right. I've adopted a few techniques to measure the quality of my relationships:

The bottomless bucket.

When I'm examining a relationship, I imagine that I'm pouring my love and energy into a bucket. I close my eyes, and

I can actually see it. My love looks like sparkling water, and the bucket is an old aluminum garden bucket with rope handles. (This is what mine looks like, but your bucket can be whatever you'd like. Maybe it's a bright blue plastic beach bucket or a wooden bucket hanging over a well.)

I've had relationships in the past (so, so many of them!) where I felt like I just kept pouring and pouring love in, yet it never filled. It was only through a great deal of reflection and therapy that I understood that many of the buckets I was pouring into had giant holes in the bottom. It didn't matter how much I put into it; it was never going to get full.

There are infinite reasons why relationship buckets get holes. I've spent endless hours trying to figure out *why* a person is never satisfied. These endless hours were just another form of my love being dumped into an abyss. It's okay to seek understanding about other people's dysfunction. Sometimes, that helps us heal. Just make sure that you are seeking understanding so that you can forgive them and not because you want to try to fix them.

You can't patch holes in other people. This is a futile waste of your time. Instead, focus your energy on patching your holes. This is the only thing you can control.

If you find yourself pouring and pouring love into someone else to the point of exhaustion, and you're never getting anything back—or worse, it seems like they are actively hammering away at your bucket, chipping out holes so that all your healthy love is draining out—then perhaps it's time to stop and think about whether this relationship is adding value to your life or the other person's. Maybe it's time to set some boundaries to extract yourself from the shame cycle.

Apply the circumstances to a neutral party.

Another of my favorite ways of holding myself and others accountable is to imagine myself having the exact same interaction with other people. Often, when we are caught in the middle of a shame cycle, we are too close to even recognize what's happening. If we pull ourselves outside of the cycle and apply the same circumstance to a neutral person (real or imagined), sometimes this will help the light bulb turn on over our heads and illuminate the situation.

Here's an example:

You have a friend who wants to have lunch every single Wednesday. You enjoy having lunch with her, but sometimes you have scheduling conflicts—a deadline at work, a child home sick, a flat tire, whatever.

When you must cancel, which is very infrequently, your friend becomes passive-aggressive. She calls and texts every hour all day, telling you how much she misses you, how she has so much she needs to talk about, or explaining how much harder and more hectic her day was than yours.

You end up feeling so guilty that the next time you have a scheduling conflict, you cancel it and show up to your usual lunch date, even though you're feeling resentful and stressed.

We've all had this sort of interaction at one point or another. Guilt is one of the ugly ancestors of shame (along with anger, humiliation, abandonment, and pain). To extract yourself from this shame cycle, mentally remove the other person from the situation and replace them with someone with better boundaries. If you can't think of a specific person, make one up. In your mind's eye, literally pluck the other person out of their seat at the table, and plop someone else down in their place.

How does this new person react to your cancelation? Is she understanding? Sympathetic? Does she wish you sincere luck on your big project at work? Inquire genuinely about the health of your sick child? Does she offer to come help you change your tire or pick you up from the service station while your car is getting worked on?

Let's move back even further. Considering your full, busy life, is a once-a-week lunch date even reasonable? Maybe it is. In which case, great! But maybe it's not. Maybe you don't just resent the guilt trips on occasions you have to miss, but you resent the entire premise. You have other friends you'd like to have lunch with, and you only have the funds or the time to go out to lunch once per week. Maybe once a month is a more reasonable expectation. Or maybe, this relationship needs to be put on hold entirely, either permanently or temporarily, until you have a better handle on just how toxic this situation has become for you.

What if you're the one with a hole in your bucket?

I have some bad news for you. We all have a few holes in our buckets. Those holes manifest in different ways for different individuals. Sometimes, they show up as emotional distancing. (This is my fatal flaw.) Sometimes, they show up as guilt trips or gaslighting, or other forms of manipulation.

It's crucial that you dig deep to recognize your holes, your toxicity. Because until you know the holes are there, you can't get to work repairing them. Imperfection is okay. There is no shame in weakness. There is only shame in being too much of a coward to admit it. (I know. Ouch! But somebody had to say it.)

It's never too late to hold yourself and others accountable.

It's true that the longer you wait, the harder it may be to attain accountability. Once we become accustomed to living in a situation, even if it is highly toxic, it can feel safer to stay where we are than risk the conflict and discomfort of developing new, healthier norms.

But remember, "We can do hard things."[6] I would argue that accountability is not optional. It is a *necessity* for the well-being of yourself, your family, and even the toxic people in your life, particularly if there are children involved. Kids who grow up in shame cycles and toxic circumstances are starting off miles behind their peers with emotionally healthy childhoods. I discuss this more in Chapter 13.

Accountability takes intention and maintenance.

Once we have redefined love, setting boundaries and holding others accountable becomes a lot less scary. Even though the other person still may not see it as a good thing, within yourself you know that you are sharing your whole, honest self. And you don't have to be angry or aggressive about it because you understand that boundaries are an act of love.

By admitting that we are all capable of good and evil, we become more prescient to the toxicity of others. Our judgment becomes clearer. We can recognize that although this person is doing a lot of good in the world, they may not be the best for us. We can also recognize good in others where many can't see it. We love each person individually.

The reward for embarking on this journey is peace within yourself. You will know who you are and where you stand. You will have self-respect where once there had been shame. Seek the support you need to become accountable, and bravely step into accountability knowing that a balanced life is waiting for you on the other side.

Loving with accountability.

When I began my redefining love journey, I found holding myself and others accountable to be so deeply difficult. It required me to determine what my boundaries are and then hold myself and others to those boundaries. I had to constantly check my intentions, and it seemed that I failed more often than I succeeded.

When I set boundaries, I felt like I was being *mean* to people. Sometimes, I was so insecure about my right to live a separate, healthy life that my boundaries became too rigid and unforgiving. Conversations I went into with a clear head and the best of intentions descended into defensiveness and raised voices. Very often, I'd slip back into unhealthy patterns, especially within my most deeply enmeshed relationships.

There is an enormous learning curve to the process of redefining love, which is why it is so important to surround yourself with at least a few healthy, supportive, objective friends or loved ones who can walk this journey with you. You need someone who will honestly hold you accountable, who will call you out when you are slipping back into old patterns, and who will celebrate with you when you do well.

For me, in addition to supportive friends and family, my therapist was crucial in helping me set boundaries within my toxic relationships. She cheered me on when I was afraid, held me accountable when I didn't handle things as well as I should have, and helped me recognize when I regressed into old habits.

Once I redefined love, I began making meaningful connections with other emotionally healthy people. Just as shame
cycles can snowball, dragging in other vulnerable people
nearby, so too can healthy connections grow exponentially.
Don't hesitate to seek extra help if you ever need a little support while processing your relationships.

Six

GRACE

*"By judging others we blind ourselves to our own
evil and to the grace which others are just as
entitled to as we are."*

Dietrich Bonhoeffer

IN REDEFINING LOVE, IT IS CRUCIAL THAT WE SEE
the equal capacity for good and evil in ourselves and others.
When we have accepted that every one of us has within us
light and darkness, we can recognize that a person may be
a blessing to one and a curse to another. We can then allow
others their journeys, which is Grace.

When we redefine love, we love everyone, regardless of
their actions or beliefs. Since we are not required to be in
close relationship with anyone, we can love from a distance
when necessary. We can accept blessings from someone who
has hurt others (as we all have) and allow others to appreciate
the blessings offered by those who have hurt us.

Grace allows us to view conflict not as a negative to be
avoided but as an opportunity to better understand another
person. Perhaps we have something to learn from them, and
they from us.

Grace is the foundation of forgiveness. When we can accept that a person's actions reflect deep grief and hurt, we can forgive and *set ourselves free* to move on with our lives. Grace allows us to take our power back from others by severing the ties of bitterness, rage, and shame.

What grace is not:

Grace is *not* a free jerk pass. Grace is *not* blindly burying our heads to injustice or wrongdoing. Grace is *not* a complimentary ticket to the inside of our heads and hearts. Grace is *not* an excuse to ignore bad behavior. Grace is *not* a reason to excuse away toxicity. Grace is *not* resigning yourself to being mistreated, bullied, or abused.

What grace is:

Grace is the ability to look at someone's shortcomings with compassion and empathy. Grace is the willingness to accept that we all grow at our own pace. Grace is the love we hold for everyone, despite our differences. Grace is the peace we find when we allow others their paths. Grace is the self-respect we feel despite our flaws.

Grace is the foundation for our boundaries. Grace is the guidepost against which we harness the gate we can choose to hold open or respectfully close depending on how others fit into our personal voyage through life. Grace is the window we look through when we redefine love.

Create a love spiral.

The answer to all brokenness, whether it is ours or someone else's, is love. Loving yourself despite your mistakes, shame, and insecurities sets you free to love others. Loving others despite their shortcomings sets you free to love yourself. It is a new spiral—a love spiral.

You can't fix everyone. But you can work on yourself and teach your children a new way to love and be loved. And perhaps you might influence others in your life as they see your newfound confidence and happiness.

PART THREE
APPLYING THE PRINCIPLES

SEVEN

FORGIVENESS

"The weak can never forgive.
Forgiveness is the attribute of the strong."

Mahatma Gandhi

OUR CULTURE IS CONFUSED ABOUT FORGIVENESS. On the one hand, we are told that we must forgive others to move on, and that is absolutely true. On the other hand, we are told to "forgive and forget." If we forget the wrongs done to us, we don't retain the lesson. If we don't retain the lesson, we are doomed to repeat the same mistakes in future relationships.

Culture is also confused about what forgiveness looks like. Forgiveness is identified by culture as "standing by your man," "friends are forever," and the family welcoming back the returning prodigal son.

But what if standing by your man (or woman) is dangerous to you or your children? What if, by returning time and again, you are enabling a person to continue on a self-destructive path? What if your absence from the person's life is the wake-up call they need to make better choices? What if the person is better served by your loving from a distance, whether they see it that way or not?

And what if the prodigal is not the son who left but the person who drove him away in the first place? What if the recklessness is generational, and the son was simply carrying on a family tradition of excess and dysfunction that he learned in his youth?

The greatest confusion in our culture about forgiveness is propagated against us by the least likely to take responsibility. Manipulative people would like us to believe that forgiveness, love, and trust are the same thing.

And because we want to believe only the best about people, we believe them. And in doing so, we keep coming back, over and over, enabling the least accountable to continue behaviors that are damaging to not only us but also themselves.

We take this incorrect notion of forgiveness and use it to judge others. We see people setting boundaries and assume they can't forgive. Perhaps that is the case in some instances. But perhaps the person has learned that, in this case, with this particular person, loving from a distance is far more compassionate. Perhaps the person has simply redefined love.

Forgiveness redefined.

In the Redefining Love Framework, forgiveness, trust, and love are three entirely separate concepts:

Love is not always warm regard and affection. Love requires accountability for yourself and others. Love requires boundaries in which you clearly define where you end and the other person begins. Our capacity for love is infinite, but our time and energy are not. We choose our close relationships with *intention* based on mutual respect for boundaries.

Trust is the gift of our time, energy, and affection given to those we have welcomed into our self-made family. The level of trust given is directly correlated with the level of respect given for our expressed boundaries.

Forgiveness is the peace we feel when we have held ourselves and others equally accountable for the wrongs done in the relationship, when we have freed ourselves from the shame cycle associated with the relationship, and when we love ourselves and the other person *despite* past wrongs.

The path to forgiveness.

Forgiveness has absolutely *nothing* to do with time, attention, or affection. Redefining love requires respect for everyone's chosen path. You can do this from a distance if someone's choices violate your boundaries, integrity, or personal and emotional safety.

In *Redefining Love*, forgiveness and love are not the same thing. However, forgiveness is a crucial component in *Redefining Love*. When we redefine love, forgiveness will naturally follow. We can't love someone and harbor anger and resentment. And since *Redefining Love* involves accountability and boundaries, we aren't allowing other people to walk all over us in an effort to forgive.

Redefining love is possible regardless of what the other person did, no matter how painful. Once we have loved ourselves through our anger, we are able to see that this person is caught up in their own shame cycle. This person is full of sadness and uncontrolled anger of their own. We feel empathy and compassion for them.

Redefining love allows you to love people from a safe distance. If someone is toxic in your life, it's okay to withhold close relationship, not because you hate them (even if the other person says that is the case), and not because you can't forgive (also a highly likely response when firm boundaries are set). You respect others' rights to be in whatever place they are at any given moment. But you also respect yourself enough to recognize that you are in a different place.

In *Redefining Love*, you make your own family (see Chapter 13). This doesn't mean you must dissolve your relationship with your family of origin. It is quite possible that you will *choose* your family of origin to share your life with. The point is that your relationships should be *intentional*. You should know exactly *why* you are spending time with a person.

Toxic people use guilt, obligation, and coercion to manipulate your feelings. They try to convince you that you are unforgiving and cruel if you do not allow them access to your life. By equating forgiveness, trust, and love, they hope to blur the line between where you end and they begin. They seek to entrap you back into the shame cycle. Don't fall for it!

Forgiving yourself.

Remember that a crucial element of *Redefining Love* is learning to love yourself. A major component of this is self-forgiveness. This means admitting what you've done to harm others, loving yourself through it, and releasing yourself from the shame cycle you've been punishing yourself with for so long.

We are all flawed creatures. We have all made mistakes. Treat yourself with the same grace you would your best friend. Don't talk to yourself with derogatory and demeaning language. Our brains will believe the words we speak to them. If we call ourselves stupid, worthless, or disgusting, our brains will believe it.

Close your eyes and imagine yourself as a child. Now try telling that innocent child all the horrible things you tell your adult self. It's almost impossible to imagine. You would never allow anyone to speak to a child that way, so why are you allowing yourself to speak to *you* that way?

(If you think it's okay to talk to a child that way, see Chapter 11 on toxic relationships. It's time for some personal accountability.)

Permission to love and be loved from a distance.

Obligation, guilt, and coercion are terrible reasons to expend your limited time and energy on a relationship. I am officially giving you permission to choose to love the toxic people in your life from a distance.

You have a right to decide for yourself what your boundaries are in each individual relationship. This includes your family of origin. If your parents, siblings, and other family members are toxic to you, it's okay to set boundaries. It's okay to tell your adult children, "No."

It's okay to expect your spouse to respect your individual needs and identity. It's okay to put some distance between yourself and that friend from high school who still wants to party every night. It's okay to find a new mom group if you feel judged. It's okay to skip out on the latest gossip session at work. It's all okay.

What these boundaries look like is entirely up to you, and they may evolve over time. You may decide to cut off communication for a time until you feel stronger and more able to enforce your boundaries. You may choose to limit your time to once a week or once a month. You may choose to only meet a person in a public place. You may even choose to discontinue the relationship with a person for the remainder of your life.

That being said, this only works if you've built a solid foundation for redefining love. If you haven't been accountable for your actions, if you haven't held the other person accountable, if you are still screaming at each other and you shut someone out of your life simply for spite, if you aren't consistent with your boundaries and are constantly changing the rules of the relationship, then you are still in a shame cycle, and you certainly have not redefined love.

We have a responsibility to those we love, and we love *everyone,* regardless of their toxicity. Our responsibility is to know ourselves well enough to set firm boundaries for a healthy life and to respect others' boundaries as well. We must give ourselves permission to let go of relationships that are not serving a healthy purpose in our lives.

We must also allow other people to let us go. We must forgive ourselves for the hurt we've caused and acknowledge that other people have a right to love us from a distance that feels safe to them.

EIGHT

SPEAK THE LANGUAGE

*"When people talk, listen completely.
Most people never listen."*

Ernest Hemingway

I HAVE ALWAYS BEEN ADEPT AT READING FACIAL expressions, at figuring out the silent messages people are sending with their body language, at seeing beyond their spoken words to what they *really* want to communicate.

I credit this in large part to my upbringing in a dysfunctional home. (There truly are benefits to everything if you're willing to think outside the box!) I grew up tiptoeing around on eggshells, trying not to rock the boat, trying to anticipate others' moods so I could react accordingly.

The truth is, we can speak the same verbal language and still not understand a word someone else is saying. Try sitting through the worship service of a religion other than your own. Or teenager humor. Or old people humor. Or profession-specific humor.

I once worked in the corporate offices of a large dental insurance company. It took me months to understand dental insurance humor. But once I did, it was funnier than a root canal at an underwriter's convention. (That one gets me every time.)

What I've learned by paying attention to the subtleties of human behavior is that we *all* speak our own languages. We *all* come from a world that only exists inside our heads and hearts.

Accept that we are all different.

It certainly would be simpler if everyone saw things exactly as we do. But that doesn't work on several levels. First, how boring! Second, that's simply *not the way it is*. Why whine about something we can't change?

The first step in learning to speak someone's individual language is to accept that we are all different. We all see the world through the lens of our experiences, and no two lives are exactly alike. We all have our successes, failures, opportunities, and disadvantages. And we all have our own way of applying meaning to these experiences.

Accepting differences is not equal to agreement.

Accepting that everyone is different is not an endorsement of things you don't agree with. The fact that we are different inevitably means that we are going to disagree, which often leads to anger. Our knee-jerk reaction to anger is defensiveness. We automatically feel threatened, which triggers our fight-or-flight response, which makes rational problem-solving impossible.

When we attempt to speak another person's individual language, we are putting ourselves in their shoes. We are experiencing empathy. We are considering a person's set of unique experiences and seeing how these experiences have impacted who they are. If this is a person with whom we strongly disagree, empathy helps us remain calm. It helps us avoid the fear of conflict, which avoids the fight-or-flight response, which allows us to remain rational.

Empathy and agreement are vastly different concepts.

Empathy is trying to meet another person where they are in their personal journey through life.

Agreement is a hearty pat on the back and a good laugh over mutually agreed-upon values.

Redefining love does not require you to invite those with whom you strongly disagree to your house for dinner. It simply requires you to remain calm, listen, and try to understand where they are coming from.

In fact, learning to speak other people's individual languages makes it easier to set boundaries. If where they are at is not compatible with your life's path, you can choose to love them from a distance. The distinction is that where once you might have felt anger, bitterness, resentfulness, or even hatred, you can now love them *despite* your differences.

Everyone has a story.

The only way we can understand where someone else is coming from is to listen to their story. To listen to their story, we must ask questions, which automatically diffuses a situation. It's difficult to remain angry with someone who appears interested in your life. If you give someone a chance, they will help you understand why they see things the way they do.

Sometimes, highly toxic people will continue to behave aggressively or manipulatively no matter how hard you try to understand their point of view. In these cases, empathy requires more work. When direct communication fails, you must let their actions do the talking.

Look at what you know about the person's history. If we are in close relationship, we probably know a thing or two about their life experiences. Chances are, it won't take much effort to find a direct correlation between their experiences and their behavior. They may not be saying it directly, but their actions are speaking their language loud and clear.

An extreme example of this is someone who is openly racist. Nobody is *born* racist. Racism must be learned. Imagine what this person must have been through to bring them to this point. Imagine the messages they must have been sent as a child. Once, long ago, they were a helpless infant.

This person's experiences certainly don't justify their behavior, but imagining what horror they must have seen and heard in their life may help you feel empathy. You may not want to have anything to do with this person, but by loving them from a distance, you are not giving in to hate and bitterness, which just embroils you in the other person's shame cycle.

Language barriers are frustrating, but they aren't insurmountable. Whether we are dealing with someone from another country, someone across the street with a yard full of political signs that grate on our nerves, or someone in our family we simply cannot understand, we have a responsibility to try to see the world through their eyes.

In *Redefining Love*, we must try to speak each other's language. We must attempt to understand even those to whom we struggle profoundly to relate. We must respect the other person's way of expressing their boundaries and beliefs. And we must love despite even the most painful disagreements.

Once we accept the difference between empathy and agreement, it becomes easier to feel empathy. Learning to speak other people's language helps us set boundaries and find peace in even the most challenging relationships.

NINE

DEALING WITH ANGER

"Anger as soon as fed is dead—
'Tis starving makes it fat."

Emily Dickinson

IN ORDER TO REDEFINE LOVE, YOU MUST MAKE peace with anger.

Culture has trained us to believe that anger is a bad thing. Therefore, when we feel anger, we tend to do one of two things—we suppress it, or we lash out. Both actions are not only a waste of time but also a waste of a powerful force for change.

Anger can be very motivating. Anger gives us the courage to take a stand. Anger only feels bad to us because we have been taught since childhood to believe that we shouldn't be feeling that way.

To redefine love, you must make peace with anger. Anger is rooted in fear. Fear triggers a primal fight-or-flight response, and *whoosh!* Rationality flies right out the window, right along with our self-worth. So, it is crucial that we learn to deal constructively with anger. The first step to this is accepting it for what it is—a signal from our subconscious that something isn't right.

Emotions are the brain's dashboard.

Strong emotions are not bad or good. Emotions just *are*. We all have them, and they serve an important purpose. All our emotions, including those considered negative—such as anger—are there to communicate messages we need about the world.

Emotions are our nervous system's way of telling our bodies how to react. Joy tells us that this is a circumstance where we can feel safe. Excitement tells us that we are emotionally safe, but we also need to be alert. Sadness is a notification that something in our world has irreparably changed. Fear is a warning that there is danger present. Guilt is a warning that we may need to change our behavior. Anger is a warning that it's time to set some healthy boundaries.

Big feelings are very useful tools to help us navigate life. But when they malfunction, they can diminish our quality of life by generating shame, bitterness, anxiety, and depression.

Our nervous system is a complex computer.

The human nervous system uses energy and electrical currents to communicate with the rest of our body's system, like how the electrical system in a car communicates messages to the rest of the machine.

And just like a car, sometimes maintenance is required. When we experience trauma or long periods of stress, our body's internal communication system gets stuck. I look at it like a car's dashboard.

Have you ever had a warning light in your dashboard malfunction? It stays on all the time, even when there's nothing wrong with your car. It's not that the warning light is a bad thing. It's there to warn us and keep us safe. Most of us don't have the knowledge necessary to fix it ourselves. So, we take our car to a mechanic, who will reset the system.

What causes our brain's dashboard to malfunction?

Our brains are made up of an intricate system of nerves and tissue that all work together to keep our bodies moving, our emotions regulated, and our souls aligned. Just like a computer, if even one circuit is blown or one wire is crossed, it can affect the functioning of the whole machine.

Big experiences, particularly negative ones, can sometimes cause our nervous system to short-circuit. We call this *trauma*. This response can come in many forms—big traumas, small traumas, one-time traumas, or ongoing traumas.

Like everything else, trauma is relative.

Why do siblings who grow up in the same house have different memories of the same event?

Why do some soldiers from the same unit suffer from PTSD while others appear to integrate back into civilian life with ease?

Why does one witness to the same violent crime go on with life as usual, but the other is plagued by nightmares?

We are all born with our distinct temperaments, strengths, weaknesses, moods, and personalities. We'll call this your default or factory settings.

Everything that we experience from the moment we are born are downloads that fundamentally change the way our nervous system processes information and communicates with our bodies.

Since every one of us has a unique lived experience—what country you're born in, what religion your family practices, your socioeconomic circumstances, nutrition, birth order, rural versus urban, etc.—it makes sense that every individual comes to react differently to external stimuli.

Every nervous system is unique. And thus, everyone is going to react to trauma differently. An incident that wreaks havoc on one brain might not affect another brain much at all. (And, of course, we know that just because someone seems to have it all together, it's quite possible that they are suffering silently.)

This is why it is so crucial that we don't compare our reactions to life's hardships with someone else's.

You're not "crazy."

We are only in the very early stages of understanding the human nervous system. The human brain and how it relates to the rest of our body is still a mystery in many ways. The more we learn, the better we become at healing from trauma.

We don't know much, but we do know that much of what our culture has dismissed as crazy or antisocial is actually an individual's response to trauma. This is *huge* because it allows us to give grace and offer support rather than push trauma survivors to the outer rims of society with institutionalization, isolation, and incarceration.

We still have a long way to go in this area, but it's heartening to see a shift away from condemnation of mental health struggles towards a more inclusive perspective of healing and support.

We are living in an exciting time. Neurologists are constantly finding new ways to heal our brains from trauma. There are so many more tools in the healing toolbox than there used to be.

As a culture, we are finally starting to accept that mental health maintenance is as important as physical health. If one healing modality doesn't work for you, don't give up! There may be another option that could help. And just because something worked well for one person doesn't mean it's the right method for you. Remember—every nervous system is unique.

Timing is everything.

It's important to find the right sources to help heal your trauma. If you try to tighten a flathead screw with a Phillips, you'll quickly get frustrated and exhausted, and you'll still have a screw loose.

When I look back at my healing journey, I can see how different therapists and different modalities helped me at different times. When I first started therapy in the middle of a contentious divorce, I needed practical, immediate solutions to a very high-stress situation, and I needed an objective person to offer perspective to help me manage fear and stress.

Once the divorce was finalized and my life had resumed a predictable rhythm, I needed to dig in and figure out the *why* and *how* of the first thirty years of my life. How on earth did I screw everything up, and why did I allow myself to be treated so badly? It took many years to find those answers.

Once I understood the why and how, it was time to apply what I'd learned and create a new, healthier reality. I've had four therapists who served four very different purposes.

The first was a hard-nosed, plain-spoken realist who could objectively help me deal with the unraveling of what had been my reality for thirty years. It was incredibly terrifying to realize that my entire life had been a fabrication. It was a little like stepping into the *Matrix*, and without help and support, it would have been impossible to get my bearings.

My first therapist was the one who pointed out that my dashboard was broken.

My second therapist was a soft-spoken, introspective woman who walked me through the hard questions. She was trained in diagnoses and healing modalities, and she knew how to hold space for me to process all the big feelings that accompany facing hard truths. This was a lengthy, arduous process. I saw her for eight years.

My second therapist was the one who pulled off the dash face, fiddled around, and diagnosed what was wrong with my warning light.

The third therapist was practical and matter of fact. I was ready to set boundaries, but I needed an objective outside source to reinforce my new reality and hold me accountable when I slipped into old, unhealthy patterns. She gently eased me out of my comfort zone without pushing too hard or too fast.

The third was the one who reconnected the wires and got my warning light working properly again.

I am still actively in therapy with the fourth. Now that I've had healthy boundaries in place for a few years, I'm ready to grow beyond mere emotional maintenance and create a new, joyful, empowered reality that is entirely my own.

My current therapist is teaching me how to trust my brain's dashboard. After a lifetime of second-guessing myself, it's time to realize that I'm a well-oiled machine capable of great things. I anticipate this will be a lifelong process. I'm of the belief that everyone needs a therapist to support them through the ups and downs of life, much like we need a dentist to call when we have a toothache.

How do you know what you need and when?

It can be overwhelming to try to find the help and support you need to heal your trauma. Because every individual is unique, there is no hard and fast guide to finding the right therapist or coach. Therefore, community is so important.

Surround yourself with healthy, growth-minded people. You can't grow in the same toxic soil that poisoned you. In my experience, and from what I've seen in others, once you step outside of the toxic cycle and begin making relationships with others who are focused on healing and growth, the right people start flooding your life.

Resist the urge to go it alone. Trauma survivors learn early on that trusting people can be dangerous. The trouble with this is we need community to survive. Humans were not meant to live in isolation. We are pack animals. We are tribal. We need others to rely on to survive.

The first step in your healing journey is to ask for help. If everyone in your life is telling you you're crazy, that it's all in your head, that it's all your fault, or "you brought this on yourself," and not offering any tangible ways to change and heal, then it's time to seek support outside your tribe.

A sure sign of a toxic tribe is isolating those who ask hard questions. If your tribe is toxic, it's time to find a new one. This doesn't mean you have to cut everyone out of your life. Maybe that will be a part of your healing journey, but also maybe not. (We'll explore that in a future chapter.) But you'll never know what else is out there if you don't explore new connections with others.

If asking questions creates serious conflict, this is a sign that something's not quite right. In healthy relationships, there is room for disagreement. If you feel afraid to bring up a topic, get curious about why. Are you holding back because you're nervous about how others in your circle will react? Those feelings of discomfort are a signal that this may be an issue that needs to be explored.

Attempting to avoid conflict is not only a waste of time because it is impossible, but it is also a wasted opportunity for growth and change. It is not the existence of anger and conflict that matters but how we choose to manage it when it occurs.

Mindfulness.

Mindfulness is presence and intentional awareness of how you are feeling in any given moment. Mindfulness is identifying your feelings, such as, "I'm feeling happy right now," or "This person is frustrating me." This process is called *naming* your feelings.

Mindfulness requires self-talk, which takes some practice. It feels strange at first to give yourself a pep talk. Some people find it helps to write it down versus simply speaking to yourself. Once you get in the habit of examining your feelings through self-talk, it becomes habit.

There may be no better time to practice mindfulness than when you're angry. Identifying your feelings helps you slow down and reflect, which brings back rationality. It keeps anger from being the boss. (You should never let your feelings be your boss!)

Once you have brought back rationality, you can assess the situation more objectively. You can decide if you are in danger or whether this person is someone who will respect your boundaries.

During the height of anger, you are unable to make healthy boundaries. You may push people away who might have been wonderful additions to your life, or you may allow people who are toxic to remain in your inner circle.

Whether it is suppressed or expressed, anger clouds your judgment. Remember that your feelings—including anger—are a warning light on your brain's dashboard. When you feel anger bubbling up, sit with it quietly and approach it with curiosity. What is your anger trying to tell you? What is there to learn from this experience?

Don't be ashamed of your anger. Don't lash out. Don't suppress it. Just acknowledge that it's there and love yourself through it. Remember that a crucial piece of *Redefining Love* is loving yourself. Decide what is best for you in the situation. Should you set firm boundaries? Should you take a stand? Or does the situation feel less threatening once you have talked yourself through your anger?

Redefining forgiveness.

Sometimes people do horrible things, things that are very deserving of anger. (Remember, anger is not a bad thing.) But dwelling too long on anger will destroy you.

There is a lot of talk in our culture about forgiveness that is misguided. I'm not an advocate of forgiving and forgetting. Forgetting is the equivalent of denial, which is the root of dysfunction. We focus too much time on forgiving people and not enough on loving them in a healthy way.

Redefining love is less about forgiveness and more about loving the person *despite* their shortcomings. If we have fully redefined love, then forgiveness will naturally follow. We can't love someone and harbor anger and resentment. And since *Redefining Love* involves accountability, we aren't allowing other people to walk all over us in an effort to forgive.

Regardless of what the other person did, no matter how awful, redefining love is possible. Once we have loved ourselves through our anger, we are able to see that this person is full of brokenness. This person is full of sadness and uncontrolled anger of their own. We feel empathy and compassion for them.

There's room for anger *and* love.

One of the myths our culture supports is that if we love someone, we shouldn't feel big, hard emotions towards them. In reality, it is possible to feel both anger and love at the same time.

Sometimes people continue to behave recklessly or hurtfully even after we have expressed our boundaries or taken a stand. Sometimes we must remind ourselves repeatedly to love a person who continues with the same offensive behaviors.

The key is to stay in charge of your feelings. *You* choose whether love will reign or anger will be in charge. If you continue to love yourself through your anger, you will be able to maintain control of your response to your big feelings.

Manipulative people thrive on triggering your anger because they know that if you're angry, they can maintain control. By loving someone who is actively trying to hurt you, you confuse them. You take back control of your life.

Eventually, by redefining love, you'll be able to make peace with anger and love yourself and others through even the toughest conflicts.

TEN

THE SHAME CYCLE

"Shame corrodes the very part of us that
believes we are capable of change."

Brené Brown

SHAME CYCLES EXIST EVERYWHERE. NO ONE CAN escape them entirely. And shame is not always a bad thing. Shame works closely with its friend guilt to create *conscience*— the part of ourselves that keeps our integrity in check. Since none of us are perfect, we are all bound to screw up from time to time. In an emotionally healthy person, when mistakes happen, shame and guilt step in to remind us that we need to make the situation right. But left unchecked, shame can poison us and everyone around us.

The Shame Cycle.

The term "shame cycle" is not a new one. In psychology, it is usually used to describe an internal cycle of shame that starts with a bad behavior, which leads to guilt, which leads to a craving for relief, which leads you to further poor choices, and so on and so forth. Although very real and perhaps relatable to you, this is not the shame cycle we are discussing in the Redefining Love Framework.

The shame cycle in *Redefining Love* is *relational*. It has to do with how we relate to other people. In *Redefining Love*, shame and guilt are considered *contagious*. If left unchecked, it can pass from one person to another to another. This is the type of shame cycle that is referenced throughout this book.

Without accountability, shame and guilt can infect the person who feels it and all those in proximity. Entire families are infected generationally. Shame cycles can grow to affect entire companies, communities, or, dare I say, even entire countries.

A relational shame cycle starts when someone refuses accountability for their mistakes. When we refuse accountability, we become outwardly defensive and inwardly ashamed. Outwardly, we work to cover up our mistakes and align people to our point of view.

Most of us know conceptually that there are always two sides to a story. Yet, when faced with an angry, defensive person, we tend to become angry and defensive ourselves. We either side with the person who is angry or the recipient. Either way, we feel internally ashamed because we know that this situation has nothing at all to do with us.

In dysfunctional families, shame is almost always generational. People living with dysfunctional families in the 21st century probably have no direct connection to the original source of their shame. Somewhere, way back in your family's history, someone made a mistake, refused accountability, became ashamed, and *voila!* A shame cycle was born.

When we feel shame without accountability, our primary goal is to pass the buck. When a parent screams at her five-year-old child that he is stupid and worthless, it has zero to do with the child and everything to do with the parent's feelings of worthlessness.

Their feelings of worthlessness were planted and reinforced by their parents, which were reinforced by their parents, and so on... back to some caveman who fell asleep on guard duty and a saber-toothed tiger ate his sister.

No one is immune.

Unfortunately, none of us are entirely immune to shame cycles. Even the most resilient among us sometimes get drawn into the drama. We can't always avoid shame cycles, but we can learn to recognize them so we can avoid infecting those around us when shame comes knocking.

Here's an example...

Let's say you're working on a tight deadline, and someone in your office just won't stop trying to chat with you. You send out all the signals that you need to get to work. You rustle papers. You sit with your head in your hands, staring at the work spread all over your desk. You smile and nod without really listening. Maybe you don't even look at them while they are talking.

Most of us have been on the other side of this situation as well, when we were totally bored or distracted at work. You've finished all your tasks for the week, or you are really upset about something, and you just need to talk. You seek out a colleague who is normally friendly. Clearly, he is deep in thought. But still, who wouldn't be interested in your awesome weekend plans? Or how angry you are? You need a friend right now. So, you stand there and keep talking, mostly just to hear your own voice, completely oblivious to the disinterest of your listener.

We've all been on the giving and receiving end of a similar conversation. And whether you are the giver or the receiver, in both cases you are caught up in a shame cycle. Certainly not the most dangerous kind, but a shame cycle, nonetheless.

By passively listening to the other person ramble on, you are violating your boundaries, which makes you feel weak, which makes you feel ashamed. Somewhere deep within yourself, beneath the panic of trying to meet your deadline, you are flogging yourself.

Subconsciously, you are thinking, *Why can't I just tell this person I'm too busy to talk?* You become angry at yourself, which makes you feel defensive, which quickly turns to anger at the other person.

Though not communicated directly to the other person, your anger becomes clear in your posture and demeanor. Though consciously focused on the conversation, subconsciously, the other person feels insecure and unloved. A voice deep inside is saying, "I'm not worth listening to." The talker feels ashamed, which makes them angry at themselves, which makes them feel defensive, which makes them angry at you.

So, the talker moves on to the office drama queen—that one person in the office who is *always* willing to listen. They discuss what a jerk you are, what a stick in the mud, what a kiss-up to the boss, what a bad friend you are. As soon as the other person walks away, the drama queen is headed to your office.

The drama queen tells you in great, slightly exaggerated detail exactly what the other person said about you. You are already mad at them for interrupting your work. Now you are thoroughly ticked off.

But inside, you also feel kind of guilty for not listening and being a good friend to your colleague. You feel inwardly ashamed of your inadequacy. Not only were you a bad listener to your friend, but now here you are gossiping about them instead of working on your project. Now you're a bad friend *and* a bad employee!

Meanwhile, the other person is in someone else's office, or on the phone, or at a coffee shop, feeling outwardly angry at you and telling anyone who will listen while feeling inwardly ashamed because deep down, he knows he should have just let you get your work done.

And BOOM… You have a shame cycle.

Breaking a shame cycle.

When you are caught up in a shame cycle, you are both the purveyor and recipient of shame. You dish it out just as fast as you're taking it in. Two-way accountability is the only way to escape. You must hold yourself accountable for your part in the cycle and hold others equally accountable as well.

This means no gossiping, no taking sides, and absolutely no disrespecting other people's boundaries. Without *intentional* reflection on your feelings and the feelings of the other person, shame grows entirely in our subconscious, and we aren't even aware it's there.

Look at the above example. If either of the participants had reflected for a moment about their feelings and the feelings of the other person, the entire scenario would have ended quickly and without incident.

Redefining love breaks the shame cycle because it requires accountability, which requires you to look within yourself and the other person for the motivations behind their behavior. When you've redefined love, you're able to set boundaries. You're also able to recognize that the other person is struggling. This empathy prevents you from gossiping.

You don't feel guilty about setting boundaries because you realize that setting boundaries is an act of love. You are telling the other person where you end and they begin. Therefore, it isn't that you are being mean to your coworker by explaining you don't have time to talk. You simply respect yourself enough to realize you have a deadline to meet, and you respect the other person enough to be honest.

Conversely, you also realize that the other person isn't being mean to you by ignoring you when you want to talk. They have something going on that has nothing to do with you, and you should leave them to it. You love yourself enough to recognize you don't need someone else's validation, and you love the other person enough to respect their boundaries.

Of course, you can't control how the other person reacts. It is quite possible that the other person will continue with the shame cycle without you. But that is the key phrase—*without you*. Just because other people are spinning in an endless cycle of shame doesn't mean you have to be part of it.

ELEVEN

TOXIC RELATIONSHIPS

"If you ever get the chance to treat them the way they treated you, I hope you choose to walk away and do better."

Najwa Zeina

TOXIC RELATIONSHIPS AFFECT EVERYONE. WE ALL end up in one at least once in our lifetime. Although toxic relationships are a universal experience and perhaps one of the most dangerous circumstances we encounter, we rarely discuss them.

We warn our children about looking both ways before they cross the street, about not running with scissors, about stranger danger, and not walking on thin ice. But we don't teach them how to avoid destructive relationships that can scar them for life.

What is a toxic relationship?

A toxic relationship is one that poisons many, if not all, areas of your life. A toxic relationship is one where no respect for boundaries exists between you and the other person. Toxic relationships are those that distract us from our work and our interactions with all others in our lives. They seep into our consciousness when we are enjoying other people outside of the relationship and manipulate and control us from afar.

We are all capable of being toxic.

I'm going to test your ability to accept your darkness here and suggest something that may be uncomfortable. We are all toxic to someone.

Remember, a key component of *Redefining Love* is accepting that we are all made up of equal parts good and evil. Certainly, there are those who manage their capacity for evil better than others, but that doesn't mean they are *always* good or have always *been* good.

Until you have accounted for your darkness, you have no way to control it. In fact, unless you have admitted it exists, your evil controls you. By admitting that we are all capable of good and evil, we become more prescient to the toxicity of others. Our judgment becomes clearer. We can recognize that although this person is doing a lot of good in the world, they may not be the best *for us*.

We can also recognize good in others where many can't see it. We don't get trapped in unhealthy relationships by judging books by their covers. We love each person individually, and we know clearly where we end and the other person begins.

Toxic spirals.

The danger of not recognizing our capacity for good and evil is the development of toxic spirals. It is difficult to determine where a toxic spiral begins, and it can only end with conscious effort.

Someone, somewhere in your history, was toxic to someone, who was toxic to someone else, and then someone else, and so on and so forth until it reached you. Without being able to recognize it for what it is, you unwittingly absorb that toxicity into yourself, and you pass it on to another vulnerable person, who passes it on to the next, etc.

Have you ever noticed that whole families or communities have their own "personality"? Even though the group is made up of many individuals, there is some sense of oneness or sameness about the whole that defines it. This is why we can move to a certain town and never quite fit in, or conversely, we find a place that inspires us and motivates us, and we never want to leave.

The opposite of a toxic spiral is a healthy spiral. By redefining love, you are setting yourself and your family on a health spiral that will inspire others for generations.

The toxic family.

When enmeshment, codependency, and a lack of accountability have pervaded for generations, entire families can become toxic. The individuals within the family may be able to maintain a measure of health in their outside relationships, but within the family system, no one escapes the dynamic.

For deeply dysfunctional families, the health displayed to the outside world is only an illusion. Nothing is impossible, but it is a rare occurrence that an emotionally healthy individual will rise from a deeply dysfunctional family system without intense, intentional effort to create new habits of relating to the world.

If you are a part of a toxic family, redefining love will probably not be well-received by other members of the system. Toxic families have a culture of silence that supports the toxicity generationally. Family members truly know no other way of being. Your decision to violate the silence by speaking up, holding yourself and others accountable, and setting boundaries where none previously existed is not likely to go over well.

As you begin to redefine love, you may be called crazy, selfish, or cruel. You may be asked why you have to be so difficult. Change is scary, and your newfound confidence and outspokenness are very different from how things have been in the family for generations.

If you aren't sure whether you are in a toxic family or not, you will soon discover it as you take the first steps towards redefining love. A huge red flag is when everyone in the family seems to have opinions about who you are and what you're doing, but few, if any, have asked you directly to explain yourself. Gossip and drama are key components of toxicity.

Traits of toxic individuals.

Gaslighting is perhaps the primary trait of a toxic person. Gaslighting is a form of manipulation in which the target is made to question their observations, perceptions, and intuition by being fed constant contradictions to obvious reality.

Any time someone tries to tell you how to feel or questions your experience, they are gaslighting you.

If someone tells you, "You aren't scared!" or "I did *not* make you feel that way!" they are gaslighting you. How can they possibly know how you *feel*? Only you know how something made *you* feel.

Toxic people call you crazy, or some variation of this. This is a tricky one. Sometimes toxic people have mental health struggles of their own. This is when it becomes *crucial* that you be accountable. You don't want to get into the most toxic circular argument of all, which goes something like this:

"You're crazy!"

"No, *you're* crazy!"

"Am not! You're way crazier than me!"

When I was sorting through my toxic relationships, I found the objective assessment of a trained counselor very helpful. I would ask my therapist routinely if I handled a situation appropriately, how I could have improved, and whether I was showing any signs of mental illness.

It helped so much to have an objective professional tell me that I was on the right track, that I was not crazy (as I was being told), and to have guidance as to how I should proceed when faced with highly manipulative individuals. It also helped me maintain accountability. Remember, you are just as capable of being toxic to others as they are to you. *Stay on top of it!*

You are called petty, selfish, or mean. The thing to keep reminding yourself, over and over, is that setting and maintaining boundaries is an act of love—love for yourself and love for the other person. When we set boundaries, we are showing who we truly are, independent of everyone else.

There are going to be people who don't like this new you. Your boundaries are going to be threatening to them, particularly those who have a lot invested in things staying the same. They are going to try to talk you out of your stance by insulting you. ("You are a terrible son!" or "I guess I assumed you actually *cared*!")

Remind yourself that the other person is hurting, love them where they are at, and decide that you deserve better than being in close relationship with this person, at least until they can come to a healthier place.

Remember, there is nothing petty about standing up for yourself. There is nothing petty about setting healthy boundaries. Dismissing someone's feelings as mere pettiness is one of the most common tactics toxic people use to avoid taking responsibility for their actions.

They will tell you they know you better than you know yourself. This is, of course, ridiculous. It doesn't matter if the person birthed you from their own loins or has known you since the day you were born, or has been married to you for twenty years, or whatever your connection. *No one knows you better than you know yourself.* Variations of this include, "You don't know what's good for you," and "You don't know what you want."

They don't listen to reason. This is another tricky one that requires accountability on your part. If you are screaming obscenities at a person, it isn't fair to expect them to listen. Ensure that you are not being equally toxic in the relationship. Get professional help from a licensed therapist if you need help learning how to relate in a healthy, productive way.

Once you are certain you are being calm and rational, you will know you are in a toxic relationship if the other person is still screaming obscenities or simply chooses to completely ignore or dismiss your boundaries. Whether someone is raging in anger or suffering in solemn silence, they are toxic to you if they choose to completely disregard your boundaries.

They make you feel guilty. Guilt can be a healthy emotion. Sometimes guilt helps us do the right thing or right wrongs we have already done. But in toxic relationships, guilt is abused.

If you have done the hard work of being accountable and are setting healthy boundaries in a relationship, you shouldn't feel guilty.

Remember that there are no victims in redefined love. You love everyone equally. You simply choose where you end and others begin, and you maintain those boundaries. The only one a toxic person is a victim of is themselves and their shattered sense of self.

They build an army against you. Toxic people are deeply insecure. When someone stands up to them, they see it as a threat. No matter how lovingly you set your boundaries, they are going to view you as an enemy.

A toxic person views boundary setting as a declaration of war. In war, battle lines are drawn, and everyone takes a side. Toxic people become obsessed with amassing others to their side.

Be careful here! It's tempting when someone is gossiping about you and aligning others against you to react in-kind. Don't! Recognize that the other person is hurting and scared, but don't engage in the drama. If you do, you become equally toxic, and it is impossible to redefine love.

There is a purpose.

Every relationship has a purpose in your life. Just because someone is toxic, it doesn't mean you can't learn from the experience of knowing them. In fact, if you don't learn from every single relationship, you are wasting valuable opportunities for growth.

In redefined love, you love everyone, even those who are difficult to love. Toxic people are a product of shame cycles that began long before they were born. They have been generationally poisoned by the shame of people they haven't even met. When you can recognize toxic people as *receivers* of shame as well as givers, it is easier to feel compassion for them and love them *despite* their toxicity.

Just remember, love is not equal to forgiveness, but love does *lead to* forgiveness, which is crucial for your emotional well-being.

An act of courage.

Toxic people can be very intimidating. And toxic families can be downright terrifying. If you've toed the line your whole life, suddenly deciding to "out" your toxic family is not going to go over well. It's normal to feel scared when you start setting boundaries where none existed, with people who have zero concept of what a boundary even is.

The biggest pushback will be from those who stand to lose the most. The more toxic the person, the more resistant they will be to redefined love. But know that there will be those who respect what you're doing, even if they don't yet have the courage to stand up for themselves. It is entirely possible that you will inspire others to heal, which is a beautiful thing indeed.

Toxic people will gaslight you and try to change your reality. ("You don't love me, or you wouldn't be shutting me out like this!") They will immediately get on the phone and social media and start recruiting other family members and friends to take their side.

Don't let someone else decide your truth. Don't let anyone intimidate you into compromising your integrity or your boundaries. Remind yourself over and over, "Just because they say it doesn't make it true."

Love yourself enough to stand your ground and love the other person enough to maintain your boundaries. How will they ever grow and change if nobody ever stands up to them?

Learn to let go.

We have a responsibility to those we love, and we love *everyone,* regardless of their toxicity. Our responsibility is to know ourselves well enough to set firm boundaries for a healthy life and to respect others' boundaries as well. We must give ourselves permission to let go of relationships that are not serving a healthy purpose in our lives.

We must also allow other people to let us go. Sometimes, that is more challenging than letting go of those who have harmed us. It involves being truly honest about how we have hurt others, which is never an easy task. It hurts our pride to admit that we have been toxic to other people.

Few of us intend to be toxic. By redefining love, we can accept that other people have a right to be wherever they are. If someone decides they are at a different place, we must respect their boundaries. We can also accept that those who hurt us are in their own place, and we can love them from a safe distance.

Remember, redefined love is not equal to forgiveness. They are two separate things. You can love someone without trusting them, and you can love them without forgiveness. But more than likely, once you feel safe within the boundaries of the relationship, forgiveness will naturally follow.

PART FOUR
Making Connections

Twelve

The Health Connection

"It's not the stress that kills us, it is our reaction to it."

Hans Selye

WE LIVE IN A HIGH-STRESS CULTURE. THE VERY nature of capitalism demands more work and less fun. Before the internet, we competed with our neighbors to have the nicest cars, the most well-manicured lawns, the biggest diamonds in our wedding rings, and the brightest holiday displays every December. Social media has taken it a step further to comparing our every meal and vacation.

The current divisiveness of our political climate is making things worse. An American Psychological Association survey found that 52 percent of Americans reported the 2016 presidential election was somewhat or a significant source of stress.[7] Findings were basically equal for both Democrats and Republicans.

The same study found that social media is a significant source of stress, with avid users of social media reporting higher stress levels than those who avoid it. The inception of cable news and the twenty-four-hour news cycle is also correlated to higher levels of stress nationally.

Excess cortisol.

There is an increasing awareness among physicians and psychologists of the relationship between stress and illness. A quick Google search for "stress and disease" or "stress and autoimmune disease" delivers hundreds of articles and studies on the subject.

Stress causes the release of a hormone called cortisol,[8] which, among other things, regulates our immune response. Cortisol is also what triggers our fight, flight, or freeze response, which was great back when we had to react quickly to an attack from a prehistoric predator. It has proven less useful in the age of technology and couch potatoy.

The biological process of fight or flight was originally discussed in a 1936 article in *Nature* magazine by a Canadian biochemist named Hans Selye of McGill University in Montréal. In it, he explained that without a physical reaction to the fight-or-flight response, cortisol levels build up in the blood and cause all kinds of crazy. (That's my paraphrase added for flair.)[9]

The cavemen had little time or mental capacity to worry about interpersonal relationships. Their biggest cortisol release required a physical response—either fight or flee. The physical exertion of these tasks rid the bloodstream of excess cortisol and brought back balance within the body.

The things that scare us nowadays are usually more subtle, like emotionally complex conflicts that we either quietly endure or verbally lash out against. When we don't physically respond to a threat, we deny our body the opportunity to release the excess cortisol. Therefore, it is so crucial to exercise, particularly during times of high stress.

When applied to the right circumstances, the fight-or-flight response is a healthy, normal reaction to stress or fear. However, when cortisol levels don't return to normal after a stress event due to a lack of physical exertion, especially if this repeatedly happens over an extended period, illness is sure to follow.

Since cortisol is responsible for both our immune response as well as our fight-or-flight response, it makes sense that when our cortisol levels are off balance due to high stress, our immune system becomes out of balance as well.

Dangers of chronic stress.

Research has shown that chronic stress creates a constant slow drip of extra cortisol in the bloodstream. Studies done on veterans suffering from PTSD,[10] as well as adults who experienced prolonged childhood trauma,[11] show the dangers of living with prolonged stress.

The body is highly adaptable. Eventually, it will try to compensate for this hormonal imbalance and becomes addicted to the high level of cortisol. Have you ever known someone who appeared to be addicted to drama? This may be more than merely a relatable colloquialism.

After a while, our bodies become more comfortable in this heightened state, and we are physically unable to relax. Numerous studies done on abused children and adults who were abused as children have found that heightened levels of cortisol over a long period of time *change the DNA* of children as they grow, altering their ability to adapt to stress or respond to it appropriately as adults.[12]

Most children of abuse* learn early on that there is no use speaking up; their voices won't be heard anyway. They learn to disappear so as not to upset the abuser. They live lives of silent fear, never letting their guard down and thus never leaving the fight-or-flight state. Their cortisol levels are through the roof, even after years away from their abuser, and their DNA is permanently altered. [13]

*It's important to note here that "abuse" doesn't just mean physical or sexual violence. Emotional abuse can be equally damaging and just as terrifying. It is also worth noting that *all* toxic relationships, whether you are an adult or a child, create a fight-or-flight response. Toxic relationships are *toxic*, meaning they are poisonous to our bodies on a cellular level.

When we are faced with challenging relationships, whether it be in our interpersonal lives or dealing with strangers we disagree with, we automatically feel stress and anger. Divisive political figures, bullies at our children's schools, demanding bosses, or pushy coworkers, that guy who cuts you off in traffic—the list of frustrating and infuriating relationships we face is endless.

To redefine love, you must make peace with the big, hard feelings. Anger is rooted in fear. Fear triggers the fight-or-flight response, which triggers the release of cortisol, which over time builds up in our bodies with disastrous consequences. So, it is crucial that we learn to deal constructively with big feelings if we are to redefine love.

A healthy, new you.

Challenging times help build character and provide an opportunity to learn and grow. We all know people who have come through terrible adversity or hardship and used that experience to improve their lives and the lives of others.

If you look closely at these people, they probably have some things in common. They have made peace with their past. They have learned to recognize their value in the world. They seek to help others rather than focusing only on their own struggles. Perhaps without even realizing it, these people are well on their way to redefining love.

When we redefine love, we are not only blessing those around us by accepting them just as they are, despite our differences, but we are also creating better health for ourselves.

If you are raising children, redefining love could quite literally save their lives. Raising our children in homes filled with anger, resentment, and fear alters their cortisol levels and their very DNA structure for a lifetime. They are more likely to suffer from an autoimmune disease,[14] heart disease,[15] and chronic pain[16] in adulthood. And they don't enter adulthood with the skills they need to make healthy choices about stress and relationships.

Children raised in a household that has redefined love will enter the world knowing how to manage their stress in healthy ways, with bodies that are fully equipped to respond to life's challenges in an optimal way. It's never too late to choose health for yourself and your family.

Mental health.

Mental health is a hot topic these days. Everyone seems to be diagnosing everyone else, regardless of their knowledge about mental illness. Mass shootings, domestic terrorism, sexual violence/harassment, and hate crimes have everyone scrambling for answers.

These are important conversations we should have been having all along. To put the blame on mental illness for all these issues that are a complex mix of history, culture, politics, gender, race, and socioeconomics is dangerously naïve.

The tendency of culture to blame mental illness for everything bad that happens, especially mass shootings, distracts from the hard work of solving the problem and perpetuates the generational shame cycle of mental illness. Instead of encouraging people to seek help when they are suffering, our culture reinforces the notion that mental illness is a shameful secret to keep hidden.

Research has proven time and again that those who suffer from mental illness are much more likely to be victims of a crime than to commit one. To categorize evil as mental illness perpetuates an unfair stereotype about those who suffer from mental illness while absolving perpetrators of responsibility.

For an in-depth analysis of the relationship between gun violence and mental illness, I encourage you to read the report *Mass Shootings and Gun Violence*, published by the American Psychiatric Association and authored by James L. Knoll, M.D. and George D. Annas, M.D., M.P.H.[17]

A history lesson.

Historically, society's response to mental illness has been to pretend it doesn't exist. Mentally ill people were (and in many cases still are) an embarrassment to their families and a source of profound disappointment. This disappointment often led parents and spouses to take their anger out on the mentally ill person with verbal or physical abuse or neglect.

Well-intentioned, loving families, knowing the way society might treat a mentally ill child, would go to great lengths to hide a child's struggles from the world. Families with a history of mental illness are usually caught in intense shame cycles.

Mentally ill people were (and still are) taken advantage of, used by others for selfish gains, or institutionalized. Often, they were horrifically abused in the very institutions that were supposed to care for them. Mentally ill people are highly susceptible to sexual violence and abuse.[18]

There is a high correlation between homelessness and mental illness. It is estimated that as much as one-third of America's homeless population suffers from serious mental illness, including schizophrenia, schizoaffective disorder, bipolar disorder, or major depression.[19]

This does not include those who suffer from undiagnosed disorders such as mild or moderate depression and borderline personality disorder, in which illness is not as noticeable but just as damaging to a person's ability to cope with the rigors of life.

Although we are starting to have conversations about mental illness, there remains an enormous stigma around mental health diagnosis and mental health care. Even "normal" people who seek therapy are often stigmatized. (Are any of us really *normal*? What does that even mean?)

Men in particular are shamed for considering counseling, either by others or by themselves, since they have been culturalized to believe that talking about feelings and being overwhelmed by life is a sign of weakness. Women, too, may avoid seeking mental health care as they compete in a man's world or if they have men in their lives who "don't believe in" therapy.

Many health insurance plans still do not cover mental healthcare as a standard benefit. In circumstances where the income earner(s) in a family refuses to pay for therapy and treatment, entire families suffer needlessly due to the generational stigma against mental healthcare.

Mental illness is hereditary.

Multiple studies have confirmed that a predisposition to mental illness is passed through families via their DNA. Understanding this can help remove the stigma of mental illness as a character failing on the part of the individual. Just as a cancer risk is passed genetically, so too are depression, bipolar disorder, and other mental health disorders.[20]

And just as all people with the genetic predisposition to cancer don't get the disease, not everyone who has a genetic possibility of mental illness will become mentally ill. Mental illness can lie dormant for several generations before striking again, making it hard to trace.

Of course, there are environmental forces involved as well. Just as smoking increases your likelihood of getting cancer or eating a high-carbohydrate diet increases your risk for diabetes, so too does living with high rates of emotional stress increase your chances of suffering mental illness.

Let me be clear: A mental illness diagnosis does not absolve a person of responsibility. It does, however, provide valuable information both to the individual as well as those around them that could help when addressing maladaptive, toxic, and/or dangerous behaviors. It's difficult to solve a problem when we don't understand the cause.

With proper treatment, most people with mental illness can live fulfilling, healthy lives if given the opportunity.

Compassion versus enabling.

Let's distinguish a clear difference between compassion and enabling. Compassion is loving someone through their distress despite their struggles and shortcomings. Enabling is allowing yourself to be used by another person because you feel sorry for them. Compassion is at the heart of love. Nothing good comes from enabling.

Enabling is an insult to another's intelligence. When we enable someone, we are telling him that we don't believe he is able to take charge of his life. We enable others as much for our selfish desire to feel needed as we do from a desire to help.

If a person is struggling to care for her needs, family members and friends should set very clear boundaries about how they are willing to help. A trained mental healthcare team can help family members discern what is a *need* for the mentally ill person and what is a *want* based on the patient's fear of independence and the family's desire to feel needed.

The world is a scary place for even the healthiest people. Without a proper diagnosis, those with mental illness don't understand why they can't seem to "get it together," which breeds a shame cycle that often drags down everyone around them.

People who suffer from undiagnosed mental illness are often supported emotionally and/or financially by family members who are ashamed of their behavior or in denial that there is a problem. Unfortunately, many mentally ill people learn early on how to manipulate others into caring for their needs as a survival skill. They believe their delusions because no one has ever held them accountable. They feel justified in treating others poorly because nobody ever expected any more from them.

By enabling a mentally ill person, we are giving them permission to behave erratically and violently towards themself and other people. If a mentally ill person is going to learn to cope with life, they must be taught how to meet their needs. This cannot happen if someone else is constantly stepping in whenever they are faced with any kind of challenge.

As with all people, those suffering from mental illness need to develop confidence in their abilities. This can only come with practice and the firm, loving, gentle guidance of people who believe in them.

Families need to stop being ashamed of mental illness. Society must stop ignoring the existence of diseases of the mind. If we won't even have the discussion, then we are missing an invaluable opportunity for emotional healing.

Are you mentally ill?

During the years I was redefining love, I frequently asked my therapist: "Am I crazy?" Of course, crazy is not a term therapists use. It is a derogatory term that does not bring healing. What I was really looking for was whether I showed any signs of mental illness.

We are culturalized to believe that any kind of negative emotion means we are losing it. We doubt our sanity even when we are simply experiencing the normal ups and downs of life. Sometimes life is *hard,* people!

Then again, if you are continually feeling emotionally off balance, it's worth looking into. To be truly accountable, we must be willing to explore all possibilities. There is no sense suffering in silence when there is so much help available.

A great time to reach out for support from a therapist is when you are trying to extract yourself from toxic relationships or a shame cycle. Toxic people often have mental health struggles of their own.

When I was sorting through my toxic relationships, I found the objective assessment of a trained counselor very helpful. I would ask my therapist routinely if I handled a situation appropriately or how I could have handled things differently.

Only a trained mental healthcare professional can make an accurate diagnosis of mental illness. Be careful not to be an armchair psychotherapist to yourself or others. If you have concerns about your mental health, or that of a loved one, seek professional help.

Be wary of labels.

There is a large camp of mental health professionals and lay-people who are uncomfortable with labeling someone with a specific mental illness. There is solid evidence that labels can be used against the people they are meant to help.[21]

Of particular concern is how insurance companies, law enforcement, and learning institutions will use these labels against people. Even family members may discount the thoughts and opinions of an individual who has been diagnosed with a mental illness or disorder. Toxic families using tactics like gaslighting are particularly at risk for abusing a mental health diagnosis. These are valid concerns and should not be dismissed.

Like everything else in the Redefining Love Framework, this issue must be approached with a priority on balance. If too much emphasis is placed on the label, you run the risk of losing the individuality of the person, and they become nothing more than a list of symptoms. However, if the possibility of mental illness is dismissed entirely, the person may miss out on valuable resources that could help them heal.

If you encounter someone with mental illness, whether in your personal or professional life, be careful not to dehumanize them. Try to get to know each person you encounter as a whole person worthy of love and respect.

And, if you have been diagnosed with a mental illness or disorder, surround yourself with a loving, supportive community that sees you as a uniquely special person with gifts to share with the world. It is suspected that mental illness is sorely underdiagnosed.[22] The fact that you have a diagnosis only means you have a better understanding of the challenges you face, whereas others may not.

Relationship with someone with mental illness.

Dealing with a mentally ill person can be extremely challenging, particularly if it is someone in your immediate family. Sometimes, it may feel impossible to love the person at all.

Children who grow up with a mentally ill parent enter the world with a skewed definition of relationships and the world around them. They are taught maladaptive life skills from their earliest days. Even adults who enter romantic partnerships with mentally ill people may, over time, begin to view the world through the eyes of their unhealthy partner.

When a person is finally removed from the situation, the first emotion felt is often anger—anger at the other person for causing so much pain and anger at oneself for putting up with it.

Before we can redefine love, we need to address our big, hard feelings. If you are feeling angry, you are unable to make healthy decisions about where you end and the other person begins. Be mindful of your feelings, love yourself through them, and get real about your and the other person's shortcomings.

Is it *their* fault they are mentally ill? No. But nobody has a right to treat you with disrespect.

On the other hand, is it *your* fault they are mentally ill? No. Therefore, it isn't your job to clean up after them every time they act out. Nor should you have to silently endure mistreatment because the other person has a mental illness.

How is your silence helping the situation? Are either of you happy? Are either of you growing? If not, it's time to make a change.

The tough business of setting boundaries.

A major part of *Redefining Love* is deciding with whom we want to share our whole selves. There is only so much of us to go around. Emotionally healthy people choose to share their whole selves with those who respect their boundaries because their boundaries are essentially who they are.

In some cases, we must make the hard choice to end relationships with mentally ill people. And sometimes, we just want to change the dynamic, so it is less invasive and unhealthy.

Changing the dynamic of relationships with mentally ill people is often difficult. Because the person is not mentally well, they may react irrationally to the relationship changing, and further compound the anger of the person trying to make the change.

Remember, as you begin redefining love, the mentally ill person is likely terrified. If you are close to the person, you probably have a codependent relationship. Perhaps you are their biggest enabler, the crutch they've leaned on for years. When that crutch is removed, inevitably they will fall. Who wants to fall?

What if...?

As you begin to change the dynamic of your relationship with a mentally ill person, your mind will run through every worst-case scenario. What if she turns the rest of the family against me? What if the whole world thinks I'm selfish for taking a stand? What if he harms himself or someone else?

As for people turning against you, if you are a part of a deeply enmeshed and dysfunctional family and you are the only one willing to address the elephant in the room, there is very likely going to be some pushback from other family members. That pushback may come in the form of open criticism, but in many cases, you will simply be ignored.

Take note of how this feels. Somewhere, underneath all the chaos they're creating, this is how the mentally ill person has felt their entire life. They are constantly generating drama so that people will notice they need help. Use this awareness to help you feel compassion for them.

Mentally ill people can be very intimidating. Everyone is so accustomed to walking on eggshells that the notion of taking a stand is unfathomable. Therefore, having a therapist is so important. When you're feeling insecure or tempted to back down, your therapist will remind you that you are on the right track.

Focus on seeking out support from others who are separate from the situation. See Chapter 13 about how to make your own family.

If you feel that someone is a danger to themself or others, *do not violate your boundaries and run back to the relationship*. **Call 911**. If the person is truly dangerous, you will have performed a public service. If the threat was made to test your boundaries, they'll know you mean business. If someone doesn't want 911 called on them, they shouldn't make threats about safety. Lesson learned.

In many cases, our worst fears are never realized. What if, when finally left to fend for themself, the mentally ill person surprises everyone and flourishes? If you hadn't made the choice to step back and set some healthy boundaries, you would never have known what they were capable of.

A note on personal safety.

Most people with mental illness are not dangerous. Those who are dangerous are more likely to do self-harm or to lash out in frustration or fear towards a specific individual.[23]

Try to separate the individual from their illness. When a mentally ill person behaves dangerously, it is their illness talking. It is a cry for help.

Trust your gut. If you feel unsafe, get out of the situation. Remember that *Redefining Love* is about accountability and setting boundaries. Sometimes, we must love people from a distance. There are people trained to deal with mental illness. Utilize their expertise. Seek their guidance. And above all, keep yourself and others safe.

Redefining Love for the mentally ill.

Once we have redefined love, setting boundaries and holding others accountable becomes a lot less scary. Even though the other person may still not see it that way, within yourself, you know that you are sharing your whole, honest self with them. And you don't have to be angry or aggressive about it because you are sharing an act of love.

There are always going to be people who are harder to love than others. Love may not be the first emotion you feel when you encounter a mentally ill person. Sometimes, it may take weeks, months, or years to come to a place of love for someone who behaves so erratically. But it is so incredibly worth it. Love feels a lot better than disgust, bitterness, and despair.

In a world with so much pain and discord, it's easy to wonder how just one person can make a difference. By creating emotionally healthy environments in our families, we are making the world a safer, happier place.

If there is mental illness in your life, whether it is a serious case or a more subtle personality disorder, you could change the world by holding yourself and the other person accountable, setting boundaries, and helping the mentally ill person learn to rely on themself to navigate life in a healthy way.

If you don't have mentally ill people in your life, you can help by removing the stigma from mental healthcare. You can love others who are different, who act out, who seem strange, or make you uncomfortable (from a safe distance, if necessary). You can offer love and support to friends who are struggling with a relationship with a mentally ill person.

When we redefine love, we hold ourselves accountable for our discomfort and judgment of others, and we hold others accountable for their healing. We take responsibility for our mental health and seek the help we need to ensure we are not generating shame cycles. We offer safe environments for people to admit their struggles. We remove the shame associated with mental illness. We set loving boundaries, and we maintain them.

THIRTEEN

THE FAMILY CONNECTION

"We are ghosts or we are ancestors
in our own children's lives."

Bruce Springsteen

OUR CULTURE COMMUNICATES MANY POWERFUL
messages about family. Here are just a few ways that family
is defined by culture:

There's no place like home.
Nothing is more important than family.
Daddy's little girl.
Mama's boy.
Mother knows best.
Call your mother.
Family is everything.
A dad is a hero.
A mother is sacred.
Siblings are your first friends.
Because I have a sister, I will always have a friend.
Brothers are best buddies.
Family, where life begins and love never ends.

These types of statements are beautiful and meaningful to those who grew up in happy, well-adjusted families. But what about those who didn't? For millions of people, these sorts of statements, and the images reinforced by advertising and the media, are a constant, painful reminder of what they are lacking.

Cultural gaslighting.

As we learned in Chapter 11, gaslighting is a form of manipulation in which the target is made to question their observations, perceptions, and intuition by being fed constant contradictions to obvious reality. Gaslighting is one of the primary weapons used in toxic families and relationships.

Advertising also commits gaslighting against its target audience. Popular media has been committing gaslighting against us since its inception. Every time we are told that something is healthy when it's not, or a stereotype is reinforced by a sitcom, we are being gaslit into believing that is the reality, even when intuitively we have our doubts.

For those who are products of dysfunctional families of origin, the messages received from the culture about what family is supposed to be are in stark contrast with what they observe inside the walls of their house.

Where the heart is *not.*

For many people, home is most definitely *not* where the heart is. What toxic families really need is to dig deep into their dysfunction, admit where there is both good and evil, and be accountable together. They need to redefine love to make space for big, hard feelings and conflict. But culture doesn't support this process.

Culture doesn't allow for the possibility that, for many, Christmas has nothing to do with a giant glazed ham in the center of a long table surrounded by a happy, smiling family wearing matching sweaters. Our culture is uncomfortable with the notion that some families couldn't survive ten minutes crammed together in an RV, much less a trip to Yellowstone Park.

Even when a dysfunctional family is portrayed in popular culture, by the end of the episode, everyone is hugging, or the audience is laughing because the notion of such dysfunction is so absurd, or a muscled cop is confronting an abusive spouse and taking away the rest of the family to a safe, warm place where they can start a happy, shiny new life. Justice is served in under fifty minutes.

The result of this cultural deception is that families strive to outwardly meet a standard that is inwardly impossible. Even healthy families fall into the perfection trap, made even worse by social media, where Facebook, Instagram, and Pinterest set the bar even higher.

For those in dysfunctional families, the cost of this deception is even greater. It feels hopeless to imagine a life free from drama and discord, and it feels lonely when it appears on the outside that everyone else has a perfect life.

Ideally, everyone in a dysfunctional family would heal together. Everyone would join in the process, reflecting on their strengths and shortcomings and setting and respecting healthy boundaries. But we've already established that, despite what popular culture wants us to believe, we don't live in an ideal world.

In the real world, dysfunctional families are highly resistant to change. The dysfunction is usually generational. The problems started long before we were born and, if left unchecked, will go on long after we are gone.

Make a choice.

It is very difficult to maintain a healthy sense of self within the confines of a dysfunctional or enmeshed family. And although it would be great if everyone could heal together, the truth is, that rarely happens. So, you have a choice to make. This choice is going to be different for everyone depending on their unique circumstances.

You must consciously decide where your place is within this family. You must decide what your relationship will be with each individual. *Who you really are* needs to be carefully considered and expressed. You must be intentional with the decision. Take notes or keep a journal if it helps. Meet with a counselor to guide you. Do whatever it takes to get healthy and stay healthy.

Some individuals might decide to keep firm boundaries with some members of the family and allow others a closer relationship. Or you may choose to attend a few special events throughout the year, such as holiday celebrations, weddings, and funerals, for example. What works for one person may not work for another, so it is important that you check in with yourself regularly.

In the case of highly toxic families, you may realize that there is no way to maintain your sense of self while maintaining any connection whatsoever. This can be a very lonely decision, especially since many of these people have spent their whole lives believing that family is everything and, thus, made few meaningful connections outside of their family of origin.

Make your own family.

Intention versus obligation.
In *Redefining Love*, we get to choose who we allow into our inner circle. There is a whole wide world out there. Why

should our families be limited only to those into which we were born? Regardless of whether you grew up in an emotionally healthy environment or are a product of dysfunction, we all have a right to define our family.

Making your family isn't about turning your back on your family of origin. It is quite possible that you will *choose* your family of origin to share your life with. The key to **Redefining Love is that your relationships should be** *intentional.* **You should know exactly** *why* **you are spending time with those with whom you choose to be in close relationship.**

Making your family is about choosing your relationships with intention rather than feeling bound by obligation. If you are allowing people into your inner circle out of a sense of obligation, guilt, or coercion, that is a terrible reason to expend your limited time and energy.

Loving from a distance.

Redefining love allows you to love people from a distance. If someone is toxic in your life, it's okay to withhold close relationship, not because you hate them (even if the other person says that is the case), and not because you can't forgive (also a highly likely response).

You respect another's right to be at whatever place they are in any given moment. But you also respect yourself enough to recognize that you are in a different place.

You may *choose* to share your whole self with your family of origin, or you may *choose* to share yourself with only those members of your family of origin who respect your boundaries.

Or, in the case of some highly toxic families, you may *choose* to love your family of origin from a safe distance (across town or across the country). The key is to acknowledge that your relationships are a *choice*. And choice is a key component of accountability.

There are plenty of people in the world who will accept you just as you are. There's no point in wasting your few precious years on this earth in close relationship with people who don't respect you.

Whether you choose to love your family of origin with daily contact, occasional contact, or from a distance, you have a right to determine where you end and others begin.

Once you have redefined love, you can distinguish between your capacity for love, which is infinite, and your physical space in the world, which is limited. There is only so much you to go around, so choose carefully!

With redefined love, your family is constantly growing and changing. People come into our lives for a little while, and they are so vitally important for our growth, and you to theirs. As your life and the other person's shift—as they inevitably will—you may move in different directions. It doesn't mean you love them any less. It simply means your lives have diverted onto different paths. Perhaps you'll cross paths again someday, perhaps not.

This fluidity only works if we remain accountable. We have a responsibility to those we love, and we love *everyone,* whether they are a part of our family or not. Our responsibility is to know ourselves well enough to set firm boundaries for a healthy life and to respect others' boundaries as well. We must give ourselves permission to let go of relationships that are not serving a healthy purpose in our lives.

Each of us, if we are lucky, encounters a rare few who come into our lives as family, and they remain there for the duration. With redefined love, this only works if both you and the other person respect and maintain healthy boundaries and accountability over the long term.

FOURTEEN

THE FRIEND CONNECTION

"As you learn who you are, you can better surround yourself with friends who make you a better person, and that sometimes only happens when you disassemble old relationships."

Maggie Stiefvater

OUR CULTURE ROMANTICISES FRIENDSHIP. FROM TV and movies, we learn that we should have a handful of friends from childhood that we grow old with and share all our struggles and successes as adults.

We should make lifelong friends at every single phase of life—at every step in our schooling, at every job, at every place of worship we attend, at every street crossing. We should stay in touch with those friends for eternity, 'til death do us part. Meaning that they should all be at our funeral, elbowing each other for a chance to speak at the podium about the impact we had on their lives.

And most importantly, we are supposed to have a whole lot of friends. This was the case before Facebook, Twitter, and Instagram. But now, with the inception of social media, where once we were expected by culture to have enough friends to fill a banquet hall at our perfectly planned fairytale wedding, we now must have *thousands* of friends. Or millions if you are a Kardashian. And we should all want to be a Kardashian.

The reality is that friendships are just as varied and complex as any other relationship. Sure, there are people who maintain friendships from their childhood. And that's fantastic! But really, most people don't.

Sometimes phases of life pass, and although we enjoy them while they are happening, we move on. We *must* move on to grow. Culture makes us believe that we should leave every phase with a handful of best friends who follow us into our next phase. When this doesn't happen, we feel guilty and unlikeable, which leads to shame, which turns into a shame cycle that we take into our next relationships.

How realistic is it to make a handful of friends at every chapter of your life and then carry them into the next chapter at the same level as you'd maintained before? When we pressure ourselves to maintain friendships beyond what is healthy, we lose ourselves inside the relationship. It might *feel* like the best thing to continue forcing a connection where none remains, but in reality, you are doing more harm than good to both individuals. Sometimes people serve a permanent purpose in our lives, and sometimes they serve a temporary one.

Just because you've moved on to a new phase does not mean you are no longer friends with those who are in a different place. We all have those friends we only speak to once every few years, but when we get together, it's just like old times.

Most people enter old age with only a few close friends. If these happen to be people you grew up with, that's cool. That is a rare gift to be treasured. But is the person who enters a nursing home with her best friend from grade school a better human being than the one who enters the nursing home and becomes best friends with her bridge partner in the room next door? Certainly not.

We all have our stories, and every story has its unique set of characters and events.

Social media.

Can friendships be made and maintained on social media? Absolutely! I've met some fantastic people online through work and networking. I know I date myself when I admit this, but I still find it incredible to live in a world where some of my most treasured friends I've never met in-person.

I know of people who are housebound by illness for whom social media has become a lifeline—a window to the world. Doing life during a pandemic proved to us that the human species is highly creative at building and maintaining relationships from afar.

I'm also not talking about online dating. Although I know several people who are happily married to people they met online, this chapter is about *friendship,* not romance.

These exceptions aside, social media serves as a fun way to catch up with old friends, get to know the quirky sense of humor of that seemingly uptight coworker, and watch our friends and families' kids grow up from afar.

This does *not* equal meaningful, lifelong friendship. These are not the people who are going to rush to your side if there is a crisis, who are going to put up with you at your worst or laugh with you until tears roll down your face over some silly joke only the two of you understand.

Even if you comment on every single photo posted by every single person, that doesn't make these people your friends. It just means you have way too much time on your hands and are perhaps a bit needy for validation.

Actual friendship must be maintained the good old-fashioned way. With actual contact. In-person if possible. If not, then at least by phone or video. Or an email where you can expand on your thoughts. Even a text. I'm a big fan of the old-fashioned, handwritten letter or card. *Something* personal that says you're thinking of this person beyond a thumbs-up on his latest Facebook post.

I have a love/hate relationship with social media. It is useful in so many ways, but it is also so addicting and dangerous. It can be life sucking and distract from the beautiful, glorious world around us. Please, for the love of all things good in this world—for the love of yourself, your life partner, your real, in-the-flesh friends, your children, for God and the bountiful universe (if you're into that)—*put your phone down*, get out into the world, and live your life.

And for the record, I need to reread this section sometimes, too. The temptation is real, people. I get it.

The continuum of friendships.

I believe most things exist on a continuum. There is a continuum for mental health, sexuality, politics, spirituality, intelligence, and anything else that varies by extreme. And everyone falls somewhere on a bell curve on this continuum, with zero being one extreme and ten being the other. Most of us fall somewhere around the middle.

Friendship is no exception. Imagine a continuum where zero is no social connection and ten is your most treasured friendships. Complete strangers are zero. Your lifelong friends are ten.

Most people you know fall somewhere on that continuum on one side or the other of five, with five being people you hold in warm regard, perhaps even socialize with, and lean heavily on during difficult times, but with whom your connection fades as you move on to another phase of life.

If every stranger is a friend waiting to be met, as the saying goes, then everyone you meet has the potential to move up on the continuum at any given time. But what about down? Is that possible?

With redefined love, it is. When you redefine love, you love *everyone*, regardless of whether you know them or how much contact you maintain at any given time. Just because you and a friend have moved on to another phase of life, it doesn't mean you love them any less. It simply means you recognize that there is only so much of you to go around.

Remember that redefining love allows you to distinguish between your infinite capacity for love, and your limited time and energy. Just because you move on to a new phase of life doesn't mean the people from the previous phase cease to be important to you. Far from it!

But it does mean that you need to allow yourself to fully experience this new phase without guilt or shame holding you back.

With redefined love, your connections to others are constantly growing and changing. People come into our lives for a little while, and they are so vitally important for our growth, and we are to theirs.

As your life and the other person's shift—as they inevitably will—you may move in different directions. It doesn't mean you love them any less. It simply means your lives have diverted onto different paths. Perhaps you'll cross paths again someday, perhaps not. Or perhaps you'll maintain contact, but less frequently or in a different form, such as a monthly phone call or lunch date.

It's nice to keep in touch with old friends. Just make sure the relationship is one that is nurturing to each individual's growth. If you find yourself simply going through the motions, perhaps it's time to stretch outside of your comfort zone and meet new people. If your current friendships are meant to last, they will.

This fluidity only works if we remain accountable. We have a responsibility to those we love, and in redefined love, we love *everyone,* whether they are a part of our circle of friends or not. Our responsibility is to know ourselves well enough to set firm boundaries for a healthy life and to respect others' boundaries as well.

We must give ourselves permission to let go of relationships that are not serving a healthy purpose in our lives so that we have enough room to make new connections as well as maintain those friendships that are meant to last a lifetime.

Friends as family.

As we discussed in the previous chapter, redefining love allows you to choose your family, so the line between family and friends is blurred. Your family grows as you develop new connections with people at each phase of life.

Each of us, if we are lucky, encounters a rare few who come into our lives as family, and they remain there for the duration. With redefined love, this only works if both you and the other person respect and maintain healthy boundaries and accountability over the long term.

In my experience, the closer I get to mastering redefined love, the more deep and meaningful connections I can make with others.

The Friendship Checklist.

Socializing is hard for lots of people. It's not just middle schoolers who feel socially awkward and struggle to connect with their peers. Grown-ups struggle with friendships too. The trick is to **keep it simple. Don't make friendship more complicated than it has to be.**

Here are some go-to tips to help you navigate your current friendships and build new ones:

- If someone asks you to do something—go to dinner, hang out, volunteer, schedule a play date for your kids, etc.—and you don't want to, do an internal assessment:

  Why don't you want to? If it's because you don't feel worthy of their friendship or you are afraid of making an ass of yourself, try stepping outside your comfort zone. Why would they ask if they didn't want you there?

  If it's because you already have a packed schedule, you're emotionally or physically exhausted, or something about the situation makes you feel emotionally or physically unsafe, say no. It's that simple.

- Parties are awkward for all of us! But they're still fun, so just go be awkward with other people. It's okay.

  Being nice can be hurtful. Don't tell people what you think they want to hear. Avoiding immediate discomfort only prolongs the problem and will ultimately end up harming your relationship. Be real and honest in a kind, gentle way.

- Don't yell or curse at people.

- Don't be aggressive. It takes more willpower to maintain calm than it does to lash out. Show the world how cool you are. (Think Denzel Washington. Nobody does cool better.)

- Admit when you're wrong. Always.
- If you're going to call people out on their issues, be ready to be honest about yours as well. Accountability is a two-way street.
- Give people the benefit of the doubt. We all make mistakes.
- On the other hand, if the mistakes become a pattern of behavior that is unhealthy for you, it's time to find new friends. You can still love these people from afar.
- Being vulnerable is strong and courageous. Don't be a coward. Tell people how you're really feeling.
- You can't be everyone's best friend. Be friendly to all, friends with a few.
- Put in the time. Choose the friendships that matter most and dedicate time to them.
- Make sure you aren't putting in so much time with friends that it is feeling more like a job than a charge to your batteries.

Are you living a lie? Do your friends look at your life and think it's perfect and wonderful, but when you shut your front door, it's a whole different story? This isn't honest to yourself or your friends. Get the help you need to connect with the *real you*.

Let your friends do their job. If they won't help you, find new friends. Find a church. A therapist. A shelter. A hotline. Call the police. Go to rehab. Tell your family the truth. Email me. So many people want to help you. But *do not give up*. I know it's scary. But you can do it. I promise.

FIFTEEN

THE ROMANCE
CONNECTION

"True love is not a hide-and-seek game;
in true love, both lovers seek each other."

Michael Bassey Johnson

IT MIGHT SURPRISE YOU TO DISCOVER THAT THIS
chapter is quite short. *Redefining Love* isn't specific to romantic love, and if you apply the Three Pillars of Boundaries,
Accountability, and Grace to *all* your relationships, your
romantic relationships should naturally evolve right along
with everything else.

That being said, I do have a few things to say specifically
about romantic love. Culture teaches us that romance is all
sparks and fire from beginning to end. We fall into hot, passionate love. Then we fight over petty misunderstandings.
Then we make up even more passionately than when we
first fell in love. Then we get married. Then we have a baby.
Raising kids is hard, but at the end of the day, we collapse
on the couch together and fall asleep in each other's arms.
We fight sometimes, but we always make up. Passionately.

And then we grow old together on a porch watching the sunset while our grandchildren play in our large, perfectly manicured yard. On Valentine's Day and Christmas, men *always* give women jewelry and perfume. *No exceptions.* Unless, of course, the guy buys her a car.

And finally, the most fervent message we receive about romance from culture is that we are *nothing* unless we are in hot, passionate love with someone else.

The pressure for passion is constant. Our culture is screaming, "We need more passion, people! More sparks! More steamy shower scenes! More cowbell…" (You'll only get this joke if you're a fan of early '00s *Saturday Night Live*.)[24]

I hate to be a killjoy, but redefining love isn't about passion. Passion is fleeting. Passion can feel good, but it can also be very destructive. It's quite possible to feel passion while redefining love. (In fact, I hope you do!) But please recognize that love and passion are entirely separate feelings.

One of the biggest lies culture tells us is that love and passion are the same thing. They are *not*. Not even close.

Passion is spontaneous, raw emotion. Redefined love requires mindful awareness of how you're feeling, of where you end and the other person begins. Redefined love is about recognizing where other people are on their personal journeys.

When we are falling in romantic love, the other person consumes our every thought. When we are apart, we can't wait until the next time we can be together. When we are together, we can't be close enough. We want to be constantly touching and connecting with smiles and gestures and playful banter. Falling in love is fun!

Redefining love doesn't require any real change to the process of falling in love. It just asks that you do so *mindfully*. Never forget your boundaries. Falling in love is no excuse to allow someone to violate your sense of self.

In an ideal world, everyone would redefine love *prior* to falling into romantic love. Since that isn't realistic, be aware that it is entirely possible to redefine love during a love affair. I am living proof that if you are with a partner who respects you, redefining love will only strengthen your relationship.

But be forewarned: If you are in a relationship with a person who does not appreciate you, who does not see you as a whole individual entirely separate from themselves, with your own thoughts and feelings, your relationship may not survive unless they, too, choose to redefine love.

And, even for those in a strong love partnership, redefining love can take a toll. My husband could tell you all the ways our relationship has stretched and transformed over the past decade.

This may feel scary because we fear being alone. But you can take comfort in the knowledge that once you have redefined love, healthy people will be attracted to you like a magnet. But it may take some time. (And by time, I don't mean a few weeks.)

Redefining love isn't a magic fix for all your problems. It may take years of hard work. But eventually, if you are willing to put forth the effort when the time is right and you are ready, there will be romance in your life again.

In the meantime, don't be afraid of being alone. Focus your energy on getting healthy and building a community of like-minded friends and supporters. Focus on making your family and building a life. Be your own best friend. Don't buy into the cultural message that you absolutely *must* have a life partner to be happy. That is a lie.

Be patient. Be kind to yourself and others. Be accountable. Set boundaries. You're just fine on your own.

CRUCIAL NOTE:

There is *nothing* loving about physical or sexual violence. In fact, it has nothing to do with a desire for a relationship and everything to do with the abuser's need for power and control. Physical or sexual abuse is *not* because you haven't set clear boundaries, and no amount of boundary-setting is going to end it. If you and/or your children are in danger, seek help! Reach out to someone you trust and keep speaking out until you are heard and *safe*.

Epilogue
THE BIG PICTURE OF REDEFINING LOVE

"Well-functioning people are able to accept individual differences and acknowledge the humanity of others."

Bessel van der Kolk

THE PREMISES BEHIND REDEFINING LOVE ARE not new. We know that love and relationships are messy. Most adults have some sense of accountability. Religion, philosophy, art, literature, music, and film have explored the nature of good and evil for centuries. And social scientists continue to research shame and toxic relationships.

On a personal level, like so many others, I did not dig into these topics until I was motivated by a personal crisis. When crisis struck my life, my first reaction was *fear*. This fear fueled the anger that clouded my judgment and destroyed my happiness. My response to crisis is so common. We simply aren't taught by our culture to respond with love *first*.

I want to change that. I imagine a culture where *Redefining Love* is our collective first response to the inevitable struggles of life. As the mission of *Redefining Love* states, I seek to heal our culture by healing our trauma, one individual at a time. I believe so strongly that every time held trauma is released, all of humanity heals a little.

In short, I want to change the culture. I want to change the way the human species approaches relationships and conflict. I want to end generational shame cycles, which would end generational trauma. I hold no illusions about the enormity of this task. It took us thousands of years to get into this mess. It may take thousands more to get us out. But, the sooner we start, the sooner we get there. There's no time like the present.

Navigating conflict with boundaries, accountability, and grace.

Most of us don't like taking sides, and yet so often, we do. In fact, our culture demands it. The two-party system of American politics requires that we align ourselves with either the right or left, us or them, leaving little room for compromise.

I often watch culture with the detachment of someone who, like many others, doesn't fit neatly into either extreme. A recent topic of debate in U.S. politics is whether to build a wall across our southern border to keep out illegal immigrants. I listen to these debates, and I'm intrigued. In a metaphorical sense, the wall is already there.

I've lived a city mouse/country mouse sort of life. I have experienced intense culture shock right here in my country. I can tell you, the chasm between urban and rural is vast. As is the gap between north and south, east and west, rich and poor.

Dismissing these cultural disparities is at best uninspired and at worst, dangerously naïve. **There are invisible walls already constructed all over this country.** Certainly, I can't be the only one who sees them.

It seems we live inside a mindset that any disagreement, any difference between individuals and cultures, is a bad thing. Anything that causes tension is a bad thing. *Conflict* is a bad thing. But this is all a myth.

Conflict isn't bad or good. It's just a natural consequence of free will and diversity. It's the inevitable result of a world filled with uniqueness.

At the core of this myth is the belief that to accept that someone else is different than us, we must compromise our values and integrity. But this is also untrue. Our culture's relationship with conflict is built on a toxic foundation of myth inside of myth.

We don't have to compromise our values to accept the reality that people are different. We can still argue passionately for what we believe. We just do so with the understanding that there is always going to be someone who sees things differently.

Accepting that each of us is different is not equal to agreement. The fact that we are different inevitably means that we are going to disagree. Our knee-jerk reaction to disagreements is defensiveness. We automatically feel threatened, which triggers our fight, flight, or freeze response, which makes rational problem-solving impossible.

We have been culturalized to believe that conflict is a bad thing when, in fact, it can be very constructive. Conflict is an inevitable and necessary first step to problem-solving. The only way a conflict-free world could exist is if a problem-free world existed, which will never be the case.

Problems aren't the problem. Problems are just puzzles to be solved—variations in the fabric of the human experience.

Instead of viewing problems as the root of all that is bad about the world, we should be viewing them as an opportunity to better understand ourselves, each other, and the world.

Attempting to avoid conflict is not only a waste of time because it is impossible, but it is also a wasted opportunity for growth and change. It is not the existence of conflict that matters but how we choose to manage it when it occurs.

How can *Redefining Love* be applied to culture more broadly?

Once we can accept that people are different, it becomes easier to speak their individual language. Once we understand that acceptance doesn't require agreement, we become less defensive. When we become less defensive, we can begin to redefine love. Once we've redefined love, we can start constructive problem-solving.

There are endless examples of the need for this in our culture. Anti-Abortion. Pro-Choice. Black Lives Matter. Build the Wall. Kneel For the Flag. Transgendered Bathrooms. Gay Marriage. Gun Control. Gun Rights. Me Too…

There are so many emotions behind these movements. The passion behind both sides of national and global issues is genuine and deeply rooted in culture and experience. Both sides believe fervently that they are right. We aren't always going to agree. We're just not.

When we redefine love, we accept that everyone is trying to make sense of this chaotic life in their own way, based on their experience. We can passionately disagree with others on matters of dire importance while still respecting that the conclusions drawn by others are, in most cases, coming from good intentions.

Is there evil in the world? Absolutely. But much of what we view as evil is deeply held values that differ from our own by people with as much dedication to the public good as ourselves. Imagine how different our world would be if we all stopped fearing each other and instead gave others grace for doing the best they can with the tools they've been given.

When we redefine love, it becomes easier to discern between conflicting good intentions and the truly evil. Once we become clear about the space that we take up in the world, it also becomes clear where our boundaries should be drawn. This applies to individuals, organizations, communities, and even countries.

It would certainly make things easier if we all agreed, but that's never going to happen. And I don't believe that's the way the world was meant to be. We are different *by design*. Rather than seeking to shut down the opposition with outrage, *Redefining Love* requires that we seek to hear and be heard.

Those of us living in democracies are fortunate to live in a place that offers us an opportunity to be heard. We can protest. We can publish. We can vote. We should do all these things. We should stand for something.

Protesting is a crucial right in any democratic society. But if we can't get past the protest to the necessary constructive conversations, it won't matter how many enemies we have abroad or how high a wall we build around ourselves. We will be the masters of our demise.

It is possible to feel anger and love at the same time. Sometimes, people continue to behave recklessly or hurtfully even after we have expressed our boundaries or taken a stand. Sometimes, we must remind ourselves repeatedly to love a person who continues with the same offensive behaviors.

The key is to stay in charge of your feelings. *You* choose whether love will reign or anger will be in charge. If you continue to love yourself through your anger, you will be able to maintain control of your feelings.

Manipulative people thrive on triggering your anger because they know they can maintain control when you're angry. By loving someone who is actively trying to hurt you, you confuse them. You take back control of your life!

Right now, the manipulators are thriving and laughing all the way to the bank. We must take our culture back from those who are ruling using fear. Love breeds rationality. *Be rational.*

A culture redefined.

We live in a very politically divisive time. Our politics, religions, and values are all packaged up together in a too-small suitcase, bursting at the seams. The slightest bump comes along, and *poof!* The whole thing blows wide open. Everyone's stuff gets all mixed up, and everyone is angry.

Once you redefine love, you can pack lighter. You know who you are and what you stand for. You can protect your sense of self while loving others as you recognize that those you disagree with are only trying to do the same.

What if everyone redefined love? Imagine if everyone could put their anger aside and attempt to understand where someone else was coming from.

If enough of us raise our children using the Redefining Love Framework, we could change the entire culture in a few generations. The differences between us would still exist, but the walls would come down.

Eventually, by redefining love, we would be able to make peace with anger. We would love ourselves and others through even the toughest conflicts. I see no other solution to what plagues us.

ACKNOWLEDGEMENTS

FOR ME, WRITING IS EVERYTHING. IT IS THE healing balm for all my wounds. It is my art, my magic, and my love language. How do you thank people who gave you everything? I can't. Not really. But here, I will try.

When I was 11, my gram Minabelle Olson handed me a worn copy of *Gone with the Wind* and said, "Here. You're ready for this." In hindsight, I think I may have been a bit too underfoot, complaining I was bored. So, she handed me the heaviest book on her shelf, figuring it would keep me busy for a while, which it did.

But to a little girl who felt invisible and unremarkable, it was so much more. By handing me that heavy book with over 1,000 pages, she might as well have said, "I see you, Sara. You are smart and capable. You can do hard things." I opened that book and didn't close it for thirty years.

In public school in rural Montana, USA, I learned to love the library—the smell, the quiet, the endless stories, the possibility of life outside of our small town on Highway 2. I'd have stayed in the library all day and all night if I could. It was a sacred space where I could climb into the books and be anything, or something.

I don't remember the names of any of our school librarians. But I do remember the teachers who noticed how much I

141

loved books and storytelling: Jan Mires, Mark Yoakam, Kitty Lou Rusher, Holly Heser, Sid Wilson, John Spores, Fred Fico, and Bill McWhirter. Thank you. Teachers don't get enough credit for the lives they save.

As for my journey to now, well, I'm grateful for my trauma and all who perpetrated it because without you, there'd be no *Redefining Love*, and without *Redefining Love*, there'd be no me. My life and the life of this book are inextricably linked.

And to my mentors, my team, my sisterfriends, and my heart loves, here's to you. Look what we did! It's amazing, and my whole soul thanks you.

The sisters: Becky, Jolene, Yoshie, Raquel, Britin, Jen, Anna, Kristina, Heather, and Biljana...

The mentors: Brenna, Sid, William, Karen, Jayme, Deb, Colleen, Libby, Sheridan, Deborah, and Kelli...

There's some crossover here, but you all know where you fit into the story of my life and how much I love you.

Thank you to Hailey for the editing, and the Friday Zoom crew for showing up every week to test all these theories, listen to me ramble, and share your invaluable wisdom.

Isaac, there was so much about this journey you didn't understand. I kicked you out of the room so many times because I was in the middle of a thought. You picked up the slack and made the journey possible in so many immeasurable ways. I love you, fireman.

And my boys. My *why*. The reason the cycle had to end with me. I see you. Every day, in every way. I see your beautiful souls and all that you bring to the world. May you never feel invisible. May you never wonder whether you have value. May you grow and *become* with boundaries, accountability, and grace. You are everything. Now, go create magic.

Notes

1   Merriam-Webster. https://www.merriam-webster.com/dictionary/love

2   Raszek, M. Genetics of Love. *Merogenomics*. September 2, 2020. https://merogenomics.ca/blog/en/100/Genetics_of_love

3   Frothingham, Mia. Fight, Flight, Freeze, or Fawn: What This Response Means. *Simple Psychology.* October 6, 2021. https://www.simplypsychology.org/fight-flight-freeze-fawn.html

4   Doyle, Glennon. 2016. *Love Warrior.* Flatiron Books.

5   Doyle, Glennon. 2020. *Untamed.* The Dial Press.

6   Doyle, Glennon. 2020. *Untamed.* The Dial Press.

7   American Psychological Association. 2016. *Stress in America.* http://ar2016.apa.org/stress-in-america/.

8   Mayo Clinic. *Chronic Stress Puts Your Health at Risk.* https://www.mayoclinic.org/healthy-lifestyle/stress-management/in-depth/stress/art-20046037 .

9   Viner, Russell. Putting Stress in Life: Hans Selye and the Making of Stress Theory. *Social Studies of Science.* Vol. 29, No. 3. June 1999. pp 391-410. Sage Publications, Inc. https://www.jstor.org/stable/285410.

10 U.S. Department of Veteran Affairs. *Overview of VA research on Posttraumatic Stress Disorder (PTSD). https://www.research.va.gov/topics/ptsd.cfm.*

11 DeBellis, Michael and Abigail Zisk. The Biological Effects of Childhood Trauma. *Child and Adolescent Psychiatric*

Clinics of North America. Vol. 23, Issue 2. April 2014. pp 185–222.

[12] Madhusoodanan, J. Stress Alters Children's Genomes. *Nature.* 2014. https://www.nature.com/articles/ nature.2014.14997.

[13] Jiang, Shui, Lynne Postovit, Annamaria Cattaneo, Elisabeth Binder, and Katherine Aitchison. Epigentic Modifications in Stress Response Genes Associated with Childhood Trauma. *Frontiers is Psychiatry.* Vol. 10. November 8, 2019. pp. 808. https://www.ncbi.nlm.nih.gov/pmc/articles/PMC6857662/.

[14] Stajanovich, Ljudmila and Dragomir Marisavljevich. Stress as a trigger of autoimmune disease. *Autoimmune Review.* Vol. 7 No. 3. November 29, 2007. pp 209–213. https:// pubmed.ncbi.nlm.nih.gov/18190880/#:~:text=Physical%20 and%20psychological%20stress%20has,sundry%20 stressors%20on%20immune%20function.

[15] Wojcik, Stacey and Steven Kang. Stress Can Increase Your Risk of Heart Disease. *University of Rochester Medical Center.* https://www.urmc.rochester.edu/encyclopedia/content. aspx?ContentTypeID=1&ContentID=2171#:~:text=Studies %20suggest%20that%20the%20high,plaque%20 deposits%20in%20the%20arteries.

[16] Hannibal, Kara and Mark Bishop. Chronic Stress, Cortisol Dysfunction, and Pain: A Psychoneuroendocrine Rationale for Stress Management in Pain Rehabilitation. *Journal of the American Physical Therapy Association.* Vol. 94, No. 12. Dec. 2014. pp. 1816–1825. https://www.ncbi.nlm.nih.gov/pmc/ articles/PMC4263906/

[17] Annas, George D., M.D., M.P.H. and James L. Knoll IV, M.D. 2016. Mass Shootings and Mental Illness. American Psychiatry Association Publishing. https://psychiatryonline. org/doi/pdf/10.5555/appi.books.9781615371099

[18] Desmarais, Sarah L. PhD, Kevin S. Douglas PhD, Kevin J. Grimm PhD, Kiersten L. Johnson MS, Marvin S. Swartz MD, and Richard A. Van Dorn PhD. November 12, 2014. Community Violence Perpetration and Victimization Among Adults With Mental Illnesses. American Journal

of Public Health. http://ajph.aphapublications.org/doi/abs/10.2105/AJPH.2013.301680

19   The Treatment Advocacy Center. July 25, 2014. How Many People With Serious Mental Illness Are Homeless? http://www.treatmentadvocacycenter.org/fixing-the-system/features-and-news/2596-how-many-people-with-seri ous-mental-illness-are-homeless

20   National Institutes of Health. *Looking at My Genes: What Can They Tell Me About My Mental Health.* U.S. Department of Health and Human Services. NIH Publication No. 20-MH-4298. Revised 2020. https://www.nimh.nih.gov/health/publications/looking-at-my-genes.

21   Kamaradova, Dana Klara Latalova, and Jan Prasko. July 29, 2014. Perspectives on perceived stigma and self-stigma in adult male patients with depression. *Neuropsychiatric Disease and Treatment,* 10: 1399–1405. https://www.ncbi.nlm.nih.gov/pmc/articles/PMC4122562/

22   Vermani, Monica, Madalyn Marcus and Martin Katzman. Rates of Detection of Mood and Anxiety Disorders in Primary Care: A Descriptive, Cross-Sectional Study. *The Primary Care Companion for CNS Disorders.* Vol. 13 No. 2. 2011. https://www.ncbi.nlm.nih.gov/pmc/articles/PMC3184591/#:~:text=Misdiagnosis%20rates%20reached%2065.9%25%20for,97.8%25%20for%20social%20anxiety%20disorder.

23   DeAgelis, Tori. Mental Illness and Violence: Debunking Myths, Addressing Realities. *American Psychological Association.* Vol. 52 No. 3. Updated July 11, 2022. https://www.apa.org/monitor/2021/04/ce-mental-illness.

24   Ferrell, Will. More Cowbell. *Saturday Night Live.* April 8, 2000. https://youtu.be/cVsQLlk-T0s.

About the Author

SARA BETH WALD IS A FORMER SOCIAL WORKER and journalist, blogger, and author. She is the creator of *Redefining Love*, a mindset framework that honors the struggle of deep caring and empowers us to prioritize our mental health amid conflict within relationships. Sara is passionate about holding space for trauma survivors and walking through their stories to the healing that is possible on the other side.

www.ingramcontent.com/pod-product-compliance
Lightning Source LLC
Chambersburg PA
CBHW032055040426
42335CB00037B/721